T0295348

MAKE COLLEGE YOUR SUPERPOWER

MAKE COLLEGE YOUR SUPERPOWER

It's Not Where You Go, It's What You Know

Anna Esaki-Smith

ROWMAN & LITTLEFIELD
Lanham • Boulder • New York • London

Published by Rowman & Littlefield
An imprint of The Rowman & Littlefield Publishing Group, Inc.
4501 Forbes Boulevard, Suite 200, Lanham, Maryland 20706
www.rowman.com

86-90 Paul Street, London EC2A 4NE, United Kingdom

British Library Cataloguing in Publication Information Available

Library of Congress Cataloging-in-Publication Data

Names: Esaki-Smith, Anna, author.
Title: Make college your superpower : it's not where you go, it's what you know /
    Anna Esaki-Smith.
Description: Lanham, Maryland : Rowman & Littlefield, 2024. | Includes
    bibliographical references and index. | Summary: "This book provides a new,
    innovative way for students to navigate the college application landscape. It
    shows students how selecting a college can be a strategic tool to direct one's
    future, rather than a frenzied exercise in applying to what others have deemed
    the "best" universities for everyone regardless of their career goals."—Provided
    by publisher.
Identifiers: LCCN 2023044161 (print) | LCCN 2023044162 (ebook) | ISBN
    9781538184103 (cloth) | ISBN 9781538184110 (epub)
Subjects: LCSH: Universities and colleges—United States—Admission—
    Handbooks, manuals, etc. | College choice—United States—Handbooks,
    manuals, etc.
Classification: LCC LB2351.2 .E63 2024 (print) | LCC LB2351.2 (ebook) |
    DDC 378.1/610973—dc23/eng/20231017
LC record available at https://lccn.loc.gov/2023044161
LC ebook record available at https://lccn.loc.gov/2023044162

♾️™ The paper used in this publication meets the minimum requirements of
American National Standard for Information Sciences—Permanence of Paper
for Printed Library Materials, ANSI/NISO Z39.48-1992.

To my superheroes, Sky and True

CONTENTS

CONTENTS

ACKNOWLEDGMENTS

I'd like to thank my agent Gail Hochman, who knew immediately what I was getting at when I brought up my book idea, and Christen Karniski, my editor at Rowman & Littlefield.

I owe much to Caroline Nicholas, who loves researching and writing about education as much as I do. Jennie Purvis and Eddie West have been both professional inspirations and personal friends.

I am also grateful to Craig and my family for their love and support.

And I'd like to acknowledge all the high school students out there, in the United States and overseas, anticipating the next phase of their lives. No matter the challenges that arise, keep your chin up and dreams intact.

Life is good!

PREFACE

This book is for *you*.

This book aims to empower you to find the college that will be the best fit for your unique aspirations and ambitions. How? By providing guidance, insights, and practical advice that place you within the context of the greater world.

College can represent the most exciting and stimulating time of your life. So it's important that you focus on what you want and not just follow the herd.

You're probably already being bombarded by test-taking tips and essay-writing prompts. The problem with that is that you can't see the forest for the trees, meaning that you're too bogged down with details to see the big picture.

This book will give you the forest.

Education is a transformative experience. It is a path toward self-discovery, personal growth, and acquiring knowledge that will shape your future. This book reflects that life-changing trek.

Each chapter will delve into different aspects of the college application journey, from exploring your passions and interests to figuring out a major that suits you best. Along the way, we will debunk myths, challenge conventional wisdom, and encourage you to carefully assess your choices.

This process is not just a means to an end. It's an opportunity to explore your own potential and forge your own path.

So let's begin. Open your mind, embrace the possibilities, and let the journey toward finding the perfect college unfold.

A NOTE TO READERS

Thank you for choosing this book!

These chapters contain information sourced from various reliable sources and are intended to provide general knowledge. While I have made every effort to ensure accuracy and currency, I cannot provide any warranty, whether express or implied, regarding the completeness of the information. I also do not assume any legal liability for reliance on the content, and references to third-party organizations do not constitute my endorsement.

I hope that you find the book useful in your college journey.

Bon voyage!

INTRODUCTION

The Author Confesses

Full disclosure—The author of this book, which argues that you shouldn't get hung up on how prestigious a school is, went to Ivy League schools for both undergraduate and graduate degrees.

In retrospect, I had plenty of advantages. My parents, Japanese immigrants, were very supportive of education. I can still remember the speeding tickets my mother got as she drove me up and down the East Coast as we visited a succession of universities.

But that was a different time. My yearly tuition at Cornell was around $13,000.

And I got in on a 3.28 grade-point average (GPA). Today, some estimate that Cornell's average admitted student has a 4.07 GPA.[1] My application wouldn't make the first cut. And with the total cost of tuition and room and board at my alma mater closing in on $90,000[2] a year, I'm not sure I'd even try to get in.

But going to an Ivy League school didn't make a huge difference in my life. Of course, having Cornell on my résumé got me some attention. But I failed to tap the resources available to Cornellians.

I was one of those students who daydreamed during large lecture courses. I never bothered to go to a professor's "office hours." I failed to connect with the graduate students who taught my seminars.

"It would be nice if you wouldn't look so bored," my biology teaching assistant wrote me in an assessment.

Certainly, the friendships that I made at Cornell continue to this day. That social framework, which I would have gotten in some form at any school, cannot be undervalued.

But I never sought out professors as mentors. I never pursued internships or volunteer work that might have launched me into the workforce. I didn't know what networking was.

To me, Cornell was just what I did, day-to-day. I didn't see it as a springboard to my future. I was, in short, very immature.

Despite this, during my senior year, I tried to get a bit more focused.

I bought my first suit for job interviews when employers came to campus. It was from a Calvin Klein outlet store, and I felt it gave me a professional air that I certainly didn't feel. I had majored in Asian studies with an eye toward doing something international, but I didn't quite know how to pitch myself or fully understand why someone would want to hire me.

After fielding rejections from scores of companies—from magazines to banks to big corporations—I managed to get a spot in a buyer training program for Abraham & Straus, a Brooklyn-based department store that, back in the day, had quite a solid reputation.[3] A&S wasn't upscale Saks Fifth Avenue or the then-cool Bloomingdale's, but it was a solid job offer, especially for a graduate who didn't know what she wanted to do.

On the surface, the job sounded good. If I were to make it through the training program, I'd embark on the career trajectory of a "buyer," responsible for selecting and purchasing merchandise to be sold in the store. I imagined myself being in charge of dresses and traveling to India and Indonesia to examine colorfully patterned fabrics and then to Paris and London to meet my European counterparts. I thought I might attend New York Fashion Week to get a crack at the latest designer trends or at least replicate them for a budget-minded A&S shopper.

Certainly, fresh university graduates are known to dream big, beyond the parameters of reality. And I remained full of optimism, even after discovering my salary didn't go much further than renting a sublet with a college friend in New York's then-still-affordable Brooklyn Heights neighborhood and managing my anxiety about navigating my way to downtown Brooklyn's Fulton Street, where the store was located.

But a couple of weeks into my training, my dream was pretty much kaput.

First, I had been randomly assigned to A&S's furniture department, which I had never even considered as a remote possibility. Furniture felt like a pretty clunky vehicle for a launch into the fashion world.

I learned, too, that the furniture sold at the store—chairs, sofas, and dining room tables—were often put on sale. I would be dispatched, black Sharpie in hand, to mark down the price tags on the items that were discounted.

As I worked my way across the display floor, I knew that, even though I wasn't certain what I wanted to do with my life, this task wasn't going to lead me to where I wanted to go. I wasn't interested in sales—something I should have thought about before taking this job.

My degree from Cornell's College of Arts and Sciences was meaningless in the world I was inhabiting.

Sure, I knew what I didn't want to do. That was the easy part.

But now, confronted with a blank slate, I didn't know what I actually *wanted* to do.

What followed was a sequence of jobs that were not part of any logical plan: a stint at a Japanese trading company selling rubber and a brief period at CBS, promoting their TV programs (I was really a glorified secretary).

Then I got into the Columbia University Graduate School of Journalism. It was a short nine-month master's program, and, on reflection, I could probably have learned the skills I needed by taking a job at a small local newspaper somewhere in the United States.

But Columbia had arguably the most competitive journalism program in the country. And this was back when brand meant something.

After graduation, I got a job with Reuters news agency, covering the stock market in Tokyo. The seasoned British journalist who interviewed me initially wasn't convinced I was seasoned enough for the position. But I suspect my determination and enthusiasm tipped the scales.

Eventually, I did find my way into a career I found interesting and fulfilling. But it was more through trial and error than anything else. Thinking back, I might have gotten more out of a lesser-known university had I gone in with focus and initiative.

And today, alongside shopping, there is hardly another field more disrupted by technology than journalism. Mainstream media outlets—including newspapers and magazines—have shrunk, while niche publications have proliferated.

In hindsight, I was incredibly lucky. But I also learned a lot along the way. I know what my education gave me and what it didn't give me. And I've watched colleagues from less well branded schools excel and understand why they did so.

So, as an Ivy League school alum who had graduated without concrete ideas, I can tell you how to do better. And as an education researcher who understands what the workforce needs, I can guide your way.

I personally know how contentious a battleground getting into college has become. I also understand how technology might provide you with new opportunities that were not a possibility even last year.

Today's economy is knowledge driven, meaning that what you can do will be the reason why you get a job. So now, more than ever, your future will be determined more by *what* you learn in college than *where* you went.

Going to college is a big step, and you might feel like you're already behind those who are going to "a school in Boston." But acting on knowledge and information will guarantee that you won't feel that way for long and, maybe, that you'll even pull ahead.

1

A GREAT TIME
TO BE A STUDENT

It's a *great* time to be a student.

Surprised to hear that? That's understandable. There are plenty of reasons to think the opposite.

Applying to colleges can feel intimidating. All you hear about is how hard it is to get in anywhere and that the average GPA at top universities is about a 4.0. And your parents—*yeah, your parents!*—keep harping about your "reach" schools, how you need to try harder to get into the best-known university on your wish list. Otherwise, your life is going to fall off the edge of a cliff and you might as well crumple into a ball and stay in bed.

Helping students get into an Ivy League university, the Massachusetts Institute of Technology (MIT), or Stanford has become a multi-million-dollar industry when, frankly, if you're in the running, you don't really need anything from anyone to succeed.

So what about everybody else? What about the students who just want to make the most out of college?

What about people like you?

The world has been weird these past few years. Not that it hasn't always been weird, but it's been more so than usual. The pandemic, climate change, the skyrocketing price of your *venti caramel macchiato*—it almost makes you want to brew coffee at home and carry it around in a thermos. *Almost.*

Life be lifing, as the meme goes. That pretty much sums it up.

But there's a flip side to the coin, and that flip side is pretty shiny.

So I call BS on the whole college preparation mania. And I invite you to do the same.

Let's face it—the process of applying to universities has taken whatever joy there might have been in high school and chucked it out the window. From the moment you set foot on your campus, every class, test, and quiz you take feels like a potential minefield that can blow up your college admissions game.

I'm here to tell you that it doesn't have to be this way.

Reflect on a time when you questioned or challenged a belief or idea. What prompted your thinking? What was the outcome?

This is a Common App personal essay prompt from 2021–2022. The point of my mentioning it isn't so that you can kill two birds with one stone by writing an essay draft *while* reading this book (although I guess you could).

My point is to talk about what a belief is.

Generally, a belief is something that dictates what people do.

Back in the day, people believed that women shouldn't wear pants, that men shouldn't have long hair, and that kids who didn't do well in school were just dumb.

You probably disagree with those beliefs today. Why? Because people challenged them and, in the process, created new ones. Among them: women should be able to wear pants if they want to, hair is just hair, and there are many reasons why students don't do well in school that have nothing to do with being dumb.

By questioning a belief, you expand what's possible not just for you but for others as well. Until you question your beliefs, they—not you—dictate what you are able to do.

So what would happen if you dared to challenge the belief in the college application rat race or decided that being burned out before turning 18 should not be the norm?

I'm not saying don't apply to college. According to research from the Federal Reserve Bank of New York, the average college graduate earns $78,000 a year compared to the $45,000 of their high-school-only-educated counterpart.[1]

In other words, going to college is worth it.

But isn't the belief that going to an elite university is the be-all and end-all worth challenging? Or that you are powerless when it comes to college admissions?

Don't get me wrong. Going to a highly ranked university will help you in achieving your future goals. Full stop. That credential will probably get your foot in the door of a potential employer on name value alone. And you know which universities I'm talking about—the ones your parents obsess over and your school counselor keeps identifying as your "reach schools" (if they're even on your radar at all).

Sure, at one time, not that long ago, brand mattered a lot. Those with degrees from elite universities leaped ahead of those who graduated from lesser-known schools. The Ivy League and its ilk were the gatekeepers to success.

Okay, that sounds like a big generalization, but it's largely true.

So what's changed?

Technology, pure and simple. Technology has changed everything.

Because in a world where so much is dictated by technology—how we buy clothes, how we drive (or are driven by) cars, and how we deposit checks—elite universities don't mean quite as much. In a world where innovation and ideas matter, employers care less about where you went to school and more about what you know and what you can do.

And just by being young, you know more about tech than most of the fusty professors teaching in those ivory towers. So you already have an edge in the world!

It's how you develop and optimize your skills and abilities that will make a difference in determining the course of your life.

What about looking at college admissions as a way to empower yourself?

Imagine that. Freedom from feeling inadequate when, in fact, that's the last thing you are.

Want to know a secret?

You don't need to buy into the hype. You don't need to throw a log onto that roaring admissions bonfire.

You can opt out of believing that brand is best. Brand matters only if you let it.

Step away from the frenzy and give yourself a little perspective about the future. The future—whether you go to Harvard, the State University of New York at Oneonta, or a community college—is about skills, abilities, and competencies. It's about what you can bring to the workforce no matter where you go to school.

If you have started to learn to code, if you are interested in studying cybersecurity, or if your friends are always saying you're creative and think outside the box—well, you may not need a degree from the California Institute of Technology (Caltech) to succeed. Is your strength humanities? You have even more reason to celebrate, as the ability to think, process information, and communicate has never been held at such a premium.

In today's world, there's room at the top for many. Be smart, informed, and strategic and claim your spot.

So let's get the bad news over with when it comes to college admissions. Getting into the country's most highly ranked universities is harder than ever. There are many reasons why, many of which are quite complex.

But the bottom line is this. You may have learned about "supply and demand" in a high school economics course. In this case, the "supply" refers to the number of available spots in the university. The "demand" refers to the number of applicants who want to be admitted.

In general, the more prestigious and selective the university, the higher the demand for admission. Why?

Because the perceived value of attending a prestigious university is high. Sure, there are metrics that help determine a university's high ranking, such as where graduates get jobs and the salaries that they earn. But the "value" of a limited number of these institutions has permeated the public consciousness to a degree that hides what higher education as a whole can do.

It's gotten to the point that these elite universities have been anointed as custodians to a better life and a better future.

What happens to the students who don't have the perfect academic record to apply to these schools, the ones who can't afford the tuition, or the ones who fall under both categories?

The frenzied focus on getting into the Ivy League and equally renowned universities has made those students feel as if they're behind the eight ball, even before things really get started.

Did you ever think about the reasons why you feel that way and why it's gotten so competitive?

Maybe it's the quality of the education, that what you learn at a highly ranked university versus at a less famous one will make you more knowledgeable compared to other people competing in the career that you want. Or maybe it's just that you'll get a coveted internship or job simply by being a part of an elite university's alumni network.

Those questions deserve thoughtful answers, which we will get to. But suffice it to say that more students are applying to a small group of schools, while the number of freshman spots at those schools generally has not increased in tandem.

Consider New York University (NYU).

There was a day, not that long ago, that NYU wasn't a popular choice.[2] Many students didn't want to go to a school that lacked a traditional, cohesive campus or to New York City, where crime rates were high. Parents were concerned that downtown Manhattan wouldn't be safe for their kids and that using Washington Square Park as a hangout wasn't wholesome.

NYU itself experienced serious financial difficulties and declining academic standards in the early 1970s.

But then the children of the so-called boomers, or Americans born between 1946 and 1964,[3] reached high school age. The estimated 71.6 million boomers[4]—many of whom were college educated and professional—could afford tuition fees and began focusing on getting their kids into the best universities.

At the same time, New York City had been cleaning up Times Square and reducing crime rates. As a result, universities in Manhattan garnered more attention, and NYU's popularity began to increase, helped by its efforts to raise standards and secure financial solvency. In addition, the number of international students interested in studying at NYU grew significantly, helping the university's ranking rise even further.

It's a bit of a chicken-or-egg situation when trying to figure out what came first—NYU's climb in the rankings or the perceived increase in "value" of what the university offered.[5] But either way, it's become much harder to get into NYU, and competition for places has intensified in the past decade.

NYU Acceptance Rates

Class of	Applications accepted	Applications received	Admissions acceptance rate
2026	12,810	105,000	12.20%
2025	12,199	95,308	12.80%
2024	13,000	85,000	15.29%
2023	12,307	76,919	16.00%
2022	15,722	75,037	20.95%
2021	18,520	67,232	27.55%
2020	19,000	63,702	29.83%
2019	18,500	60,322	30.67%
2018	19,000	52,000	36.54%

Source: Dhriti Chadha, "NYU Acceptance Rate | What Are Your Chances of Getting In?," *Study Abroad Blogs | All About Universities, Programs, Tests, & More!*, February 12, 2023, https://ischool connect.com/blog/nyu-acceptance-rate-what-are-your-chances-of-getting-in (June 13, 2023).

You can see that, in less than 10 years, NYU's acceptance rate went from 36.54 percent for the Class of 2018 to a super-selective 12.20 percent for the Class of 2026.

And the most current rate as of this book's writing?

After receiving more than 120,000 applications, NYU's acceptance rate has narrowed to 8 percent for the class of 2027.[6]

That's more selective than Harvard's 11.8 percent admissions rate for their Class of 1999.[7] However, during that same period, Harvard's acceptance rate has shrunk to a minuscule 3.41 percent for the Class of 2027,[8] but let's put that aside for now.

Certainly, the education you get at NYU is of extremely high quality. There are great advantages to attending school in a major city that's a hub for finance and the arts. And sure, the university built a bunch of impressive modern buildings and dormitories and hired famous faculty members for their highly esteemed business and law programs.

But how much has changed in terms of what NYU offers students in "value" in the past nine short years? Did the "value" of an NYU education quadruple as its acceptance rate fell?

Most likely, it is just a matter of supply and demand, the point being that people battle to get into exclusive universities just because so many others also want to get in. It's the herd mentality at work.

It's important to know, too, that the pandemic made things worse, essentially pouring kerosene on an already fierce flame.

Stuck at home, worried about the state of the world, students spent a lot of time on their computers noodling around college websites and, in their heads, ruminating. Maybe a parent lost their job or things had gotten harder at home both money-wise and emotionally.

As a result, making sure that one's future was secure became not only a priority but also an obsession.

With that frame of mind, students began thinking, why only apply to five universities when I can shoot for 10? Maybe 15?

Or 90? Yes, a student in Florida applied to 90 colleges and universities in the fall of 2021.[9] More recently, a high school graduate from Atlanta was accepted to 50 of the 72 colleges and universities she had applied to after spending three hours a day over four months filling out applications.[10] Another Florida teenager was accepted to 27 higher-education institutions.[11] But it kind of makes sense, considering the uncertainty surrounding us—why not do all you can to make sure you get into the best college possible?

So, as a result, universities have been flooded with applications. For example, the University of California, Los Angeles (UCLA), received around 170,000 applications for fall 2023 admission, with approximately 145,900 coming from freshman applicants, making it the most-applied-to four-year university in the country.[12]

Yet, even though so many more people were applying to select universities, the number of spots generally has not increased in the same manner.

So the competition—at least among the top, say, 100 schools in the country—remains tough. In other words, there's nothing you can change about the principles of economics or about college admissions.

But the one thing you can change is how you think about it.

There are many reasons why you should think about it differently, but the most important reason is because of the world that we live in.

We live in a world of ideas.

People are constantly looking at ways to make things easier, faster, more convenient, or cheaper. With technology serving as fuel, ideas are our engine.

Believe it or not, there was a time when you could choose only between driving your own car, hailing a taxi, or taking mass transit. Paying back a friend could be done only in cash or maybe by check. Food delivery to your home meant pizza or Chinese food.

And even with the conveniences of Uber, Venmo, and DoorDash, innovation is taking us even further—driverless cars on the road, half a billion people using Apple Pay, and plant-based burgers that "bleed" covered with cheese made from nuts and ketchup made from carrots.

You can pitch an idea about anything you want to do, and you'll find someone who will say, "Hey, go for it!" Few will ever say, "That's impossible. You're crazy."

There have never been more brass rings to grab. And being smart about where you go to college is the first step toward getting all the opportunities that you not only want but also deserve.

Sure, you need to get your house in order—grades, letters of recommendation, you know the drill. But perhaps even more important, you need to get the lay of the land so you can understand the context within which you are operating.

And that might involve ignoring just about everything people have been telling you about a university education.

People still believe in things that are outdated at best or irrelevant at worst. It might be your parents or other adults around you who act like they know what's going on. But most likely, they don't.

The world you live in is cluttered with old beliefs, like going to a famous university is the answer to all your problems and if you should fail to get into one, you won't have the advantages of those who did.

So you need to shed stale assumptions about where you should go to school. Your future won't depend on *where* you go to college. It'll be determined by what you study while you're there and what you do with what you learn.

And you won't be headed to just any old future. You'll be headed toward a future you want.

Getting rid of old ways of thinking isn't easy. Developing anything new is hard.

Have you ever moved to a new neighborhood or a new school? Then you know exactly what getting accustomed to new things can be like.

And we're not talking of a new way of thinking about *just* college. There's nothing to be gained by operating in a vacuum or pretending

CHAPTER 1

that what's going on outside of college admissions doesn't matter. A new way of thinking means better understanding what's going on in the world.

And, unfortunately, often what's going on isn't great.

The world's problems can make you feel like, in the grand scheme of things, what you're doing is as distinctive as a grain of sand on a beach. California is both flooding and burning, wars across the globe are raging, and the division between rich and poor widens by the day. And you've probably been listening to your mom complain about the rising price of a dozen eggs.

So who cares where you end up going to college?

Believe me, we all do. And you should care more than ever.

First, we need people like you to help solve the world's problems. The problems are pressing and growing, and if nothing is done about them, they will become so big that you won't be able to lead the life you want.

And this isn't a far-off futuristic scenario. It's happening right now.

Want to live in Las Vegas? Nevada, the driest U.S. state, has eight years' worth of water left,[13] meaning that the city will probably run out of water in your lifetime. Maybe you don't want to settle in Vegas, but this scenario holds true for many places in the world that are sunny and dry.

Think about snorkeling at Australia's Great Barrier Reef, one of the world's natural wonders? Due to warming ocean temperatures, the reef is dying. If greenhouse gas emissions aren't reduced, the reef could be lost within a generation.[14]

Or maybe you're more a snow bunny, dreaming about skiing in the Alps? Rising temperatures and changing precipitation patterns are putting many ski resorts in the Alps at risk, and many may be forced to close in the next few decades.[15]

And time is ticking if you want to see iconic animals in the wild. Many species are threatened by habitat loss and other human activities. African elephants, polar bears, and snow leopards all may become extinct well within your lifetime.

These examples aren't mentioned to make you sad. They are mentioned because you have the potential to use your education and experience to make the world a better place. With knowledge and technology— and ideas—you have the power to make change.

Innocent Tshilombo, a refugee who fled the Democratic Republic of the Congo to Kenya after several family members were killed, had an idea.[16] He knew that refugees around the world suffered from isolation, essentially cut off from the rest of humanity.

So, with $70 borrowed from friends, he applied for some grants and built a solar-powered internet kiosk so that he and the other inhabitants of the Kakuma refugee camp could connect to the world. He then decided to create a social enterprise organization to build solar-powered internet nodes throughout the refugee camp to provide affordable and reliable internet service.

Innocent now has twenty internet nodes and has a goal to build 100. With the help of the solar-powered nodes, many of his fellow 200,000 refugees at the camp can access the world.

All it takes is an idea, some chutzpah, and support.

But when it comes to universities, people around you will remain committed to their outdated beliefs. Clinging to the past is comforting. Sticking to the way that things have always been done feels familiar.

And if one thing changes, everything connected to it will change. You can't tip over a single domino without causing all the ones lined up behind it to fall.

It'll be hard on you, too. Sometimes it feels kind of good to worry about the things your older brothers and sisters worried about when they were applying to college, maybe even what your parents worried about then and continue to worry about now.

How about those hours spent fretting if it's better to get a "B" in Advanced Placement (AP) biology or an "A" in regular biology or whether a university admissions officer will be more impressed if you're the captain of the volleyball team or the president of your school's chapter of Habitat for Humanity?

It's kind of weirdly fun to talk those things over with your friends. It's a way to vent, to blow off a little steam when you're feeling the stress.

In addition, if you're not focused on that stuff, what's supposed to take its place?

It's not like those worries don't matter. There are just many other more significant things to think about as you start to prepare for your college journey.

You need to think big.

And that's not thinking big in terms of upping your "reach" school. That's small potatoes.

You need to get a bird's-eye view of how education connects directly with the workplace. The college application process can be a strategic tool to direct your future rather than a frenzied exercise in discouragement and disappointment.

Times have changed since your parents—or even your older siblings—went to college, and it's all changed to your advantage.

What's different?

Thanks to technology, just about everything. And I don't mention technology to launch into a discussion about studying math and engineering so that you can become a software engineer for Google. Sure, that's a great way to get a start in life, and for students who have an affinity for so-called STEM subjects—science, technology, engineering, and mathematics—we're in an era where geekdom is rightly celebrated.

But because of technology, students who excel in the humanities, writing, and the social sciences are also valued because those skills cannot be replaced by a computer. In fact, automation has increased the need for communication and expression, for people who can rise above the transitional noise, connect the dots, and convey ideas and concepts. Ideas are the currency of today's economy.

More than ever, students can base decisions on data about not only the best universities to attend but also the courses they should take. In doing so, they can acquire the skills and competencies that will not only lead them to the jobs they want but make them feel fulfilled as well.

Due to the competitive nature of university admissions, students tend to hold up a magnifying glass and inspect themselves for weaknesses. They only see what's wrong.

Instead, students should be taking a personal inventory of their strengths and desires that will ultimately determine their success. Students who pick schools that match the potential contributions they can make are more satisfied with their experiences and, ultimately, their professional outcomes.

Reading this book will help you understand what's going on beyond school and dare you to look into the future and ask yourself, *What role in society do I want to play? And how am I going to make that role a reality?*

Former *Essence* magazine editor Susan L. Taylor, described as the most influential Black woman in journalism today, says, "Whatever we believe about ourselves and our ability, comes true for us."[17]

What she likely means is that you've got a lot more control over your future than you think.

Of course, there will always be those who have advantages and influence beyond your own. Getting a degree from an elite university will give many an edge. That's just the way of the world—and money and prestige can go a long way for those born to them.

But we're beginning to see a world where people are rewarded for what they know and can do rather than for whom they were born to or the prestige of their alma mater. And the reasons for that are fundamental rather than fleeting. They are rooted in economic need.

So instead of recoiling at the thought of university admissions, make college your superpower.

By doing so, you can control your destiny.

As former president Obama said, "We are the ones we've been waiting for. We are the change that we seek."[18]

So what are you waiting for? Let's go!

2

A LOOK BEHIND UNIVERSITY RANKINGS AND THE ADMISSIONS SCENE

University tuition fees rise, acceptance rates fall, and it seems as if the Ivy League is getting more exclusive by the minute. Competition to get into the country's elite universities has never been keener.

Your public library is stocked with books telling you that you've got to ace standardized tests, kill those college essays, and pack university applications with extracurricular activities. Those books are practically yelling at you to memorize more vocabulary, insert more poignant anecdotes into your college essay, and just do more, more, *more*.

To what end? To get into the most highly ranked universities possible, of course. For decades, students—and their families—have been lured into believing that "brand is best."

And if you fail to get into your "reach" school, you end up feeling like an abysmal failure.

So let's take a minute to talk about rankings.

One of the main reasons why admissions and the application process have become so tough is because so many students are influenced by a university's rank on a variety of lists. People naturally want to go to a school as high on those lists as possible.

If a university ranks highly, it must be one of the best, right?

As you begin your college search, it would be worth understanding the context within which you are operating.

Look at a ranking, and you'll see the usual suspects in the top 10 or 15 spots—the Ivy League, Stanford, MIT, and a scramble after that between the University of California (UC), Berkeley, the University of Michigan, maybe UCLA, and so on. Maybe, on a good day, Duke University or Johns Hopkins University gets up there, at least according to the *U.S. News & World Report Best National University Rankings*. Or was that *U.S. News & World Report Best Colleges*? Or *U.S. News & World Report Best Global Universities*? No, it's definitely the *Times Higher Education World University Rankings*. Or maybe the *Wall Street Journal/Times Higher Education College Rankings*. How about the *QS World University Rankings* or the *Academic Ranking of World Universities*?

Okay, never mind. It's one of those. But, joking aside, these rankings *do* serve a purpose. For example, the *U.S. News & World Report Best Colleges* rankings weigh worthy metrics such as graduation and retention rates, class size, faculty credentials, and average alumni giving rate, among other benchmarks.[1] This is good information to know.

But the blind buy-in when it comes to these rankings has resulted in a college applications frenzy.

The numbers are breathtaking. The "best" universities are flooded with unprecedented numbers of applications, resulting in record-low acceptance rates. Harvard now accepts a mere 3.4 percent of applications,[2] significantly lower than the 5.2 percent accepted for the Class of 2020[3] but slightly higher than the 3.19 percent acceptance rate the year before.[4] Applications are also up 40 to 50 percent across the board at selective schools.

It becomes a numbers game—more applications for a fixed number of freshman places make the schools more selective. And it's not just the students who want to get into those top universities—the universities themselves have thrown themselves into the scrum.

If a university is in the top 20, it aspires to be among the top 10, and the top 10 want to be the top five. One of the ways to do that is to increase the number of applications, which results in a lower acceptance rate and can make a university more attractive. UCLA's acceptance rate was 23.5 percent in 2007 and 16.09 percent 10 years later[5] and currently stands at 9.2 percent.[6] UC Berkeley's stats are similar—23.2 percent in 2007,[7] 17.1 percent in 2017,[8] and 11.4 percent now.[9]

Part of the reason why rankings have grown so important is their role in attracting increasing numbers of international students from countries like China. Many of them have never visited the United States before and come from families who are unfamiliar with the higher-education system or perhaps don't speak or read English. For them, picking universities based on their numerical ranking is a way to ensure that they are making the "right" choices, especially when they are literally draining the family's savings to put one child through four years of higher education.

Universities benefit in other ways from the overflow of applications.

If you apply to a university, you pay an application fee. Among the 889 ranked colleges that participated in an annual *U.S. News* survey, the average application fee was almost $45. The 64 colleges and universities with the highest fees charged an average of around $78. Out of those 64, 22 asked for more than that, with Arkansas Baptist College coming out on top with its $100 application fee.[10]

Sure, some colleges and universities will waive those fees for students under certain circumstances. But a good number of students probably don't blink—at least not that hard—when confronted with the expense. Compared with the hefty cost of tuition and the battle for the privilege to pay those bills, these application fees may appear paltry.

Even your parents are probably more than willing to pay those fees for the dozen or so universities you apply to so that you can improve your chance of getting into the "best" one. And they aren't alone.

But for students for whom cost is a challenge, especially those applying to numerous different schools, these fees are likely problematic.

Now multiply those fees by the 100,000 applications a college receives. If a university charges, say, $45 per application, that's a cool $4.5 million in revenue. Those funds may be used to hire staff that thoroughly review each application,[11] which would be the correct thing to do.

But the first cut is often done by computer.

For a university like UCLA, which (like all campuses in the UC system) charges an $80 application fee—$95 for international students—the income from that activity alone is substantial.

Certainly, there are plenty of manpower costs associated with processing and assessing applications. And you'd be surprised at the time spent by university admissions teams reading your application. So those fees don't equal pure profit.

But still, you can see that universities benefit simply from getting more applications.[12] More applications not only increase the possibility of filling the places they want to fill but also automatically make the university more selective because the number of freshman spots available hasn't grown. While there are many factors that contribute to the rise of a university in the rankings, having more applications and a subsequently lower acceptance rate can boost appeal.

Now peruse the "ranking" of universities that make the most revenue from application fees. The top seven are from California.[13]

Compare that with a list of the universities that receive the most applications. Out of the top 10, five are from that top-seven list of California schools that make the most application revenue.[14]

Are you surprised?

Now that we've discussed one of the impacts of the rankings, let's examine what the rankings *lack*.

This came into the spotlight a few years ago.

In 2022, Yale University Law School withdrew from the *U.S. News & World Report Best Law Schools* ranking not because the university was frustrated with not being acknowledged—Yale had dominated the *U.S. News* rating system since the magazine began releasing annual rankings in 1990—but because the rankings' criteria did not take into account the university's efforts to support students seeking public interest or academic careers.[15]

For example, one of the criteria for the rankings is the employment of law school graduates. But certain careers aren't included. The more graduates a school produces pursuing those careers, the bigger the possibility that outcome hurts the school's rankings. According to Yale, these parameters worked against efforts to embrace a wider variety of career pathways.

Want to pursue a public interest legal career helping the poor or marginalized? That might entail receiving a public interest fellowship for a couple of years so you can get some experience. Kudos on contributing to the greater good!

And by the way, *U.S. News* officially classifies you as "unemployed."

Interested in an academic career, perhaps toward a professorship? Building a career teaching aspiring lawyers usually requires getting either a master's degree or a PhD, so a pat on the back for pursuing such a worthy path!

But *U.S. News* also labels you as "unemployed."

Yale's strengths in other areas compensated for any of these *U.S. News*-determined weaknesses, so the university had the leeway to support students interested in careers in public service or academia. But that takes effort, as students who arrive at law school with an interest in serving the public have a bit of an uphill climb. Research indicates that, historically, a trying first year being bombarded with schoolwork makes being concerned about needs other than one's own difficult.[16]

What does a world look like without qualified lawyers defending the poor and underrepresented? Are tax and corporate lawyers the only legal professions that really count?

So, from that perspective, it's difficult to envision what exactly *U.S. News* means by "best" when ranking law schools in the country. By the way, Harvard, Stanford, and a number of other universities also pulled out of the race to be the "best" law school, at least as defined by *U.S. News*.

In June 2023, Columbia University announced that its undergraduate schools would no longer participate in the *U.S. News* rankings.[17] Concern over the influential role rankings play in the undergraduate admissions process was a factor in the university's retreat.

"Much is lost in this approach," Columbia said in its announcement.

If the schools that traditionally come out on top no longer want to play the rankings game, it's likely fewer students will believe the ones that remain truly are the "best." "Best" is a pretty subjective term, too. What's best for you might not be what's best for another. Ask your brother or sister the best place to go on vacation. Disneyland? Hawaii? Miami? Paris? Sure, you can agree that those are all great places to take a break, but getting a consensus is unlikely.

So, if we're talking about the next four years of your life, don't take a magazine's rankings on what's "best" at face value.

Read the small print and then decide what's important.

Only you know what's best for *you*. It's up to you to make an informed decision.

And now, there are rankings to fit any "you" you can imagine.

Maybe you're seeking a school that will give you the best shot at social mobility. Then you should apply to California State University San Marcos, which was ranked first in the *Ninth Annual Social Mobility Index of Schools*, "driving the American Dream through their ethos and action."[18]

And if being happy is your priority (not a bad criterion), have we got a ranking for you. Want to know which school radiates the most joy? A company used Amazon's artificial intelligence (AI) facial recognition technology to analyze thousands of geotagged Instagram posts at universities across the country.

And the happiest college in the United States is Texas Christian University, with 76.47 percent of faces tagged there on Instagram appearing happy, at least according to AI.[19]

The point really isn't to poke fun at all the rankings that exist today. The point is how different the lenses are through which to "rank" what's best. And it's also important to understand how universities can direct funding toward areas where improvement can drive up their rankings.[20]

So with that bit of scene setting, let's debunk a long-enduring myth: that you can somehow game the admissions system.

Some years ago, I was giving a series of talks in Tokyo, Singapore, and Hong Kong advising students on how to apply to universities in the United States, the United Kingdom, Canada, and Australia. I had compiled a panel of experts, and among them was the director of admissions at UC Berkeley.

She was warm yet professional, her hair perfectly coiffed, her sheath dress crisp. And as much as I wanted to believe that it was me who drew the huge crowds in each city, my colleague was the real magnet.

At the close of each event, she was rushed by students and parents. Much as fans lack coherent words once in the presence of their idols, nobody had anything meaningful to say. They just wanted to make a connection, hoping that meeting the admissions lead would make a difference when it came to applying to "Cal."

In Singapore, one young man trailed her like a puppy as she was leaving, calling out possible topics for his college essay. "Do you think that's good?" he'd ask after every pitch.

Sure, I caved, too. My son was a high school junior whose teachers said had "potential." In other words, his grades were good but not a slam dunk when it came to the top schools.

Before our event in Hong Kong—where my family and I were living at the time—I arranged to have my son casually appear during our lunch break to meet my colleague. He arrived on cue. He was polite and well-spoken, his poise doing me proud. But whatever it was that I was trying to make happen didn't.

I tried, too, to make my own impression.

I had become one of "those" parents, babbling nonsense at a human being who, wisely knowing her own power, kept an intentional distance.

When my son left, I was mad—not at him, who honorably resisted being a show pony, but at myself for succumbing to that admissions anxiety even though I knew better.

First, this woman led a large admissions team. All exclusive universities have considerable admissions teams. So meeting someone like an admissions director on the road doesn't mean much if anything. If you could peek behind the admissions curtain, you'd see how hard it is for a fleeting moment to get any kind of traction on an application.

And every university has a policy. You'd be surprised at how detailed they are. It goes way beyond GPAs, extracurriculars, and recommendation letters. Admissions officers are looking at in-state versus out-of-state high school students, international versus domestic students, and first-generation college-goers versus those coming from a family of college graduates.

Is the student a graduate of an urban or a rural high school? Has the high school historically provided a stream of quality applicants?

In addition, applicants are considered in the context of all the other applicants who would make up the freshman class. So it's not only who you are but also who the people around you are.

And imagine how the needs of a large public research university—like the University of Florida—might differ from Champlain College, a private liberal arts college in Burlington, Vermont.

So, considering that context, the granularity with which students pore over their applications can be energy wasted. Certainly, at the very elite schools, what distinguishes one applicant from another could be a matter of splitting hairs.

Was this college essay more impactful than that one? Did this applicant show more leadership skills in their extracurriculars than the other?

In other words, admissions officers are trying to extract meaning from information that's presented to them on a piece of paper. And just because these reviewers are looking for factors on which to base a decision doesn't mean those factors necessarily exist.

As the saying goes, *there is no there, there.*

But, if we must, let's drill down a bit further. How important are recommendation letters? They may not count as much as you think.

And there's the question students always ask: Is it better to get an "A" in regular biology than a "B" in AP biology? Of course, there is no definitive answer to that question. The context within which students are evaluated might make a difference.

However, if we're speaking gross generalities, based on the data from the National Association of College Admissions Counselors, you might want to get that "A" in regular biology.[21]

In other words, it's hard to figure out how and why students get into the universities they do.

Certainly, applications need to be competent and essays thoughtful, but there's only so much a student can do. Time and energy are better spent thinking about what you want to get out of an education rather than obsessing over applications to schools that you might not get into.

Because you do have control over one thing, and that's making the best decisions for yourself when picking the schools you apply to.

First, there are a lot of promising signs.

Regardless of major, the number of undergraduates earning a degree has increased by 24 percent over the past 10 years. In addition, female students accounted for 58 percent of total undergraduate enrollments in the fall of 2020. Enrollment trends for female and male students were similar between 2009 and 2019.[22]

All that fretting about what parts of your application are more important than others may be becoming less pertinent, meaning that there seems to be a transition back to the good ol' basics.

College admissions officers surveyed in 2018 said that "grades in all classes" and "grades in college prep classes" were of "considerable importance."[23] No surprise there.

Strength of curriculum came next and then, significantly below, SAT and ACT scores. That's probably why those tests are becoming increasingly optional at universities across the United States.

What *is* surprising is how little admissions officers care about the following: subject test scores (AP and International Baccalaureate), interview, and work experience.

If you look at trends, the information is even more telling. Since 2008, the importance placed on grades in *all* courses has increased—by a lot.

At the same time, the importance placed on college prep courses—that is, AP classes—has also declined, possibly meaning that the admissions officers surveyed are looking for solid all-around students rather than those having completed a dozen AP classes by graduation.

As universities push for diversity, casting a wider net to offer opportunities to a bigger pool of worthy students, they are eliminating admissions metrics such as AP classes and subject-specific SATs, which can be limited largely to students who can afford them.

And while we're on the subject, can we take a minute and talk about the SATs?

Believe it or not, you, your friends, and students in general are a big business.

Something as seemingly innocuous as taking a standardized test can translate into a hefty source of income for the College Board. Student data—namely, names and personal details—are a valuable source of revenue, as universities are eager to obtain that information.[24] You take the SATs and maybe fill out a form or two, and the College Board can sell your data to interested universities via data brokers.

Why are they interested? More student names and contact details mean more ways for a university to market programs and encourage applications. And according to some experts, the more applications a university garners, the more selective they can appear to be, and that can lead to a boost in their rankings.

In addition, while more students of more diverse backgrounds may be taking AP classes, there's a difference between taking the class and doing well on the exam.[25] Only if students get a "3" or more on a five-point AP test can they potentially receive college credit. If a school consistently has students who cannot earn those desirable scores, what's the point of offering the AP?

Let's return to the topic at hand, which is trying to figure out what admissions officers are looking for.

Attempting to game college admissions is like shooting arrows at a rolling donut. It's hard, there are multiple shifting variables at play, and luck weighs heavily on the process.

As you look at the universities to apply to, don't be intimidated by the traditional measures of what's "best." You can achieve your own personal best by throwing aside traditional limitations.

I know it's hard to ignore your fellow students who are getting into those branded schools. But never think that you can't equal their achievements farther down the road or even surpass them.

Throwing in a baseball analogy in any discussion always runs the danger of being corny. *You hit that out of the ballpark! That's a home run! You really struck out, didn't you?*

But I'm going to try to give it a fresh spin (while I ask that you excuse the corny pun).

At the World Baseball Classic in 2023, Japanese pitcher Shohei Ohtani gave a pep talk to the Japanese team in the locker room before they played in the finals.[26] They were taking on the Americans, a team packed with sports superstars, including center fielder Mike Trout, outfielder Mookie Betts, and first baseman Paul Goldschmidt. Because of that sheer wattage, Team USA was given the edge to win the tournament.

Even the Japanese team—itself full of talent—was dazzled by their American counterparts. And although Japan has produced a number of world-class baseball players, their abilities were often diminished because of national differences in the sport—Japan's ballparks are more compact, the strike zone is irregular, and even the ball itself is smaller, making it easier to manipulate and spin.

But Japan's team captain, Ohtani, knew that to achieve their goal of winning the tournament, the Japanese players had to shed their feelings of inferiority toward the Americans.

"Let's stop being awed by them," Ohtani said, speaking Japanese in a quiet, measured voice. "If you're in awe of them, you can't surpass them. We came here to surpass them, to reach the top.

"For one day," he said, "let's throw away our admiration for them and just think about winning."

The result? The Japanese team won on a strikeout by Mike Trout pitched by Ohtani.

Maybe it's a bit of a stretch, but you can apply Ohtani's wisdom to today's competitive world of college admissions.

While in the midst of doing your applications, you might find yourself occasionally (or maybe more than occasionally) feeling inadequate.

You've probably got math superstars in your class and students who take every AP course possible while managing to be varsity athletes, maybe even varsity athletes who also volunteer during the weekend, conducting crafts activities with the elderly at nursing homes.

Undoubtedly, their road to a famous university seems inevitable. But, as Ohtani said, don't be dazzled or intimidated by those around you.

Don't measure yourself against others.

When it comes to applying to—and getting into—college, the only person that matters is you. And how you view success, both on campus and after you graduate, will be equally yours to define.

3

THE IMPORTANCE OF
BEING FIRST

Jack Ma, a Chinese internet visionary and cofounder of the Alibaba Group with a net worth of around $25.1 billion according to *Forbes*, disclosed the advice that he gave his son about education.[1]

"You don't need to be in the top three in your class," he told his son. "Being in the middle is fine, as long as your grades aren't too bad. Only this kind of person has enough free time to learn other skills."[2]

That kind of thinking probably feels like the opposite of what people have told you about school.

What schools traditionally have taught students is that the only way to succeed is by getting good grades and that the reason why you want excellent grades is to get into your "reach schools."

Ma's wisdom may also run contrary to what your parents have told you, which might be (1) set everything else aside and (2) focus on your GPA. What you learn outside the classroom doesn't matter.

Good thing Jack Ma thought differently. Or, more accurately, he had no choice *but* to think differently.

Ma failed his college entrance examinations—twice![3] He passed on his third try and went to Hangzhou Normal University, then a teachers' school. After graduating and starting a career as an English teacher, he says he applied to Harvard Business School 10 times and was rejected each time.

But in 1995, Ma discovered how far China lagged in terms of the internet. While searching for "beer" and "China," he found nothing, so he created a basic Web page for a Chinese translation service with a friend and quickly received inquiries about it from around the world. Experiencing the power of the internet spurred him to develop a series of technology companies, the most prominent one being Alibaba, an e-commerce platform[4]—on which you can buy beer.

When Alibaba went public in 2014, it raised $25 billion,[5] which was then the largest initial public offering in financial history. At the time of writing this, Alibaba was valued at $212 billion.[6]

Ma is now one of the richest men in China, and in April 2021, he was ranked 26th in the "2021 Forbes Global Rich List."[7] Meanwhile, his alma mater, Hangzhou Normal University, was ranked number 1,103 in the 2022–2023 "Best Global Universities" ranking by *U.S. News & World Report*.[8]

"Don't try to be the best," Ma also said. "Be the first."[9]

So what does Ma mean by that?

He doesn't literally mean that you must be the first to do something, but you need to understand how society is changing and put yourself at the front of that change.

The way the world worked in your parents' and grandparents' generations is currently being dismantled. We now operate in a "knowledge economy," in other words, an economy that is based on the exchange of ideas more than physical things. What made Ma rich wasn't selling beer but selling the idea that you don't need a physical store to sell beer.

And because of the rapidity with which technology is transforming the way we live and work, the people driving change are the ones with an ear to the ground, not necessarily the ones with a super-elite education.

Think about it. We're even beyond the success stories of Uber's Travis Kalanick (UCLA dropout) and Twitter's Jack Dorsey (University of Missouri-Rolla [two years] and NYU dropout).

The next generation of young innovators are even more diverse: brothers Martin, Meti, and Massi Basiri, originally from Iran, founders of the $3.2 billion educational technology unicorn ApplyBoard (Iran's Shiraz University and Canada's Conestoga College); Nigerian American Jen Nwankwo, founder and chief executive officer (CEO) of 1910 Genetics, a biotech company that facilitates rapid drug development (Claflin University in South Carolina); and Janice Bryant Howroyd, founder of the personnel company ActOne Group and the first African American woman to establish and own a billion-dollar company (North Carolina Agricultural and Technical State University).

On the corporate side, Texas A&M University has produced four of the CEOs in the top 100 companies on the Fortune 500 list, which is the most of any college.

The current crop of CEOs at the helm of some of the country's most prominent corporations aren't graduates of traditionally elite universities either: Thasunda Brown Duckett, president and CEO of financial services organization TIAA (University of Houston); Eric Yuan, CEO of Zoom (Shandong University of Science and Technology in China); and Ted Sarandos, co-CEO of Netflix (Glendale Community College in Glendale, Arizona).

While some of these entrepreneurial and business luminaries earned advanced degrees at branded universities, their undergraduate launchpads were decidedly accessible.

At one point, an education from an elite university—which focused on an excellent overall education—was an ideal match for corporate America. Perhaps it wasn't so much the education as it was the brand, and that match extended beyond companies—even to the White House.

President George H. W. Bush went to Yale as an undergraduate; President Bill Clinton went to Yale Law School (Georgetown undergraduate); President George W. Bush went to Yale as an undergraduate and then to Harvard Business School; President Barack Obama got his undergraduate degree at Columbia University and then went to Harvard

Law School; and President Donald Trump received his bachelor's degree from the University of Pennsylvania.

It is interesting to note that both Obama and Trump transferred as undergraduates from arguably less prestigious universities (Occidental College and Fordham University, respectively) to Ivy League schools.

Perhaps they were aware that the transfer acceptance rate of even the most prestigious universities is usually greater than for regular admission.

However, President Joe Biden graduated from the University of Delaware and got a law degree from Syracuse University. Vice President Kamala Harris earned a bachelor's degree at Howard University and then earned a law degree from UC Hastings (now known as UC College of the Law, San Francisco). They are the first pairing in the White House without an Ivy League degree since 1976, when President Jimmy Carter (U.S. Naval Academy, undergraduate) and Vice President Walter Mondale (Macalester College, undergraduate; University of Minnesota Law School) were elected.

Due to the disrupted nature of the economy and the complicated nature of running our country, perhaps even the politicians in the most powerful office in the country—maybe in the world—need skills more than pedigree.

Back when your parents were kids, the economy was based on making things, stuff like cars, washers and dryers, and furniture. We're talking factories full of assembly-line workers doing the same set of tasks, day after day, to produce physical goods.

It may be hard to believe, but for families in the 1950s and 1960s, buying a television set was a big deal! Manufacturing was big business.

Of course, it still is but to a much lesser degree in the United States. Manufacturing now makes up the smallest share of the U.S. economy since 1947.

Why?

There are several reasons. First, it's cheaper for American companies to manufacture overseas. While hourly wages for factory workers vary, they can be less than $5 in Vietnam and more than $25 in the United States.

So you can see why companies like HP and Nike have set up factories overseas.

Conversely, as countries become wealthier, they need things beyond simple necessities, beyond food and clothing, and even beyond washers and dryers. They need banking, medical services, transportation, and education.

More advanced economies have a higher share of services and need the people skilled enough to provide them.

That's reflected in more Americans getting college degrees.

In the past 10 years, the number of Americans aged 25 and older who have a bachelor's degree has increased. As of 2021, 37.9 percent of adults in this age-group had completed a bachelor's degree. Among them, 14.3 percent also went on to get a graduate or professional degree.[10]

That means a workforce with more "white-collar" jobs in which people provide services than "blue-collar" jobs in which people make things.

But today technology is changing the nature of jobs, full stop.

Manufacturing is being automated. Robots are even cheaper than paying a human being overseas to perform repetitive tasks and are usually more efficient. But automation is eating white-collar jobs, too.

We're talking about the elimination of tollbooth collectors, phone telemarketers, and bank cashiers, but also paralegals, financial analysts, and even radiologists are all professions that are being rapidly automated. Yes, even doctors are being replaced by robots or AI!

Okay, maybe that's a bit of an exaggeration. But radiologists who use AI will likely replace radiologists who do not. Sometimes even the best radiologists struggle, for example, when examining mammograms for potential cancerous growths.

But let's say we have an AI tool that has been trained on a million mammography images[11] of women of different ages and races and was informed which women had been diagnosed with cancer.[12] You can see why the algorithm's ability to predict cancer is potentially much more accurate than the doctors in clinics who see a fraction of that number of cases in their careers.[13]

So this is why the importance of where you go to college is changing. It's because the economy is changing.

Think about banking. Not that long ago, moving money around required going to a bank and filling out a paper form that you handed to a teller or, at the very least, speaking to someone on the phone. Now you probably deposit checks on your phone (if you use paper checks at all).

This is a sector that is undergoing a great deal of change. So what does it take to run one of the world's biggest banks?

Noel Quinn, group chief executive of HSBC,[14] one of the world's largest financial services organizations,[15] was educated at what is now called Birmingham City University in the United Kingdom. When he was a student, it was called Birmingham Polytechnic.[16] Polytechnics generally focus on practical and skill-oriented training, while universities offer courses on academic and theoretical topics, such as math, English, and history.

Quinn is also an accountant. The economy needs new types of leaders because we have a new type of economy.

You see evidence of this change all around you: empty retail shops because everyone now shops online, self-checkout lanes at grocery stores (which means that supermarkets are offloading the labor onto customers). And even food delivery robots, though they still can't compete with speedy bicycle delivery people.

So how has our higher-education system adapted to this quickly evolving economy?

Quick answer: it hasn't. Education systems have not kept pace with the changing nature of work. They are missing opportunities to equip students with the skills that would get them great jobs.

So, as a result, employers can't find qualified people to hire.

That might be hard to believe, considering how much tuition costs these days. But universities haven't kept up with technology. Even as technology detonates entire industries, universities remain firmly mired in yesterday.

Now think of the companies and services that play a role in your everyday life: Facebook, Google, Amazon, Uber, Airbnb, Vrbo, Venmo, Zelle, PayPal, DoorDash, and Seamless.

They are based on ideas about how best to fill the needs of people like you.

Do you think it matters where those companies' founders went to school? Do you think about whether the founder of Venmo even graduated from college when you're reimbursing your friend for spotting you $15 last Friday for your Chipotle takeout?

Let's take this discussion a few steps further by presenting a few futuristic scenarios.

SCENARIO 1

If you are currently studying art in high school, you know how hard you work on your projects. If you are involved in fashion design, for example, the number of hours you spend designing clothes and sewing those outfits is formidable.

While your school has probably provided some fabric, thread, zippers, and trimmings, you might dig into your own pocket to buy what's missing to make sure that your senior fashion show is exactly how you want it to be. Why not spruce up your collection so that it's extra enough to get noticed?

Some studies show that students at design schools spend hundreds if not thousands of dollars a year for precisely that[17]—and if not in fashion, it's for materials for sculpture, painting, and the like.

And what happens once the models have walked the runway dressed in your designs or the walls have been hung with your artwork? What happens after you've enjoyed the spotlight for a few hours?

Most likely, the collection you toiled over ends up gathering dust in your family's basement, or your drawings are packed into a portfolio and slid under your bed.

What if you could find out if your artwork is original enough to be sold? What if you figured out a way for every art or fashion student to sell their work online?

SCENARIO 2

You've decided to stop eating meat.

But you don't like tofu, tempeh, or those other bland options that often replace meat. You also aren't crazy about those plant-based meat products because there's something about the consistency and look that you find unappetizing.

Preparing fish, too, is a little hard with all those scales and bones.

What you do like—indeed, what you actually *love*—is shrimp.

You'd eat shrimp for dinner every night if you could. Seems unlikely, though, right? Shrimp has always been considered kind of fancy, like that shrimp cocktail you order when you have dinner out with your parents.

What if you could grow ethical, sustainable shrimp without antibiotics or chemicals? What if you could create an urban aquaculture farm in shipping containers that uses AI? AI would make it a true "plug-and-play" proposition—you don't need a background in farming or technology to get started.

What if you could eat shrimp like it's as common as chicken?

SCENARIO 3

You're the head of marketing for a video game company, and you're tasked with finding a way to get the most eyeballs on your ads. "We need impact," your boss tells you.

The conventional platforms—Instagram, TikTok, the entire lot—aren't giving you enough bang for your buck. And those are all starting to feel a little tired.

What if you sent drones into the sky over a big city and projected a giant QR code into the clouds? The image would loom overhead, like the "bat signal" did when Commissioner Gordon was trying to beckon Batman to come save Gotham City. The crowd below could scan the code and download the video game.

How would your boss respond to that kind of impact?

SCENARIO 4

There are record numbers of refugees fleeing their home countries due to civil wars and other forms of unrest. Many end up in camps, isolated from the rest of the world. There is little in terms of resources and much less access to technology or the internet.

Many of the young refugees have difficulty finding a sense of purpose, especially when only around 5 percent of refugees attain a university education.

Imagine a scenario where young individuals can empower themselves by accessing academic instruction, exam preparation, mentorship from current college students, and guidance throughout the college application process.

What if these services were provided by former refugees who beat the formidable odds and earned a university degree and the promise of a new life?

These four scenarios are pretty out there, aren't they?

They are, but not so far out there that they can't be realized.

In fact, all four scenarios are based on reality.

Want to sell your school art projects online? On the website Otentu .com, there's even the possibility of getting professional guidance on becoming an influencer in the competitive art world.

Shrimp as the sustainable protein of the future? That's the goal of Atarraya Inc, a food tech start-up.

Drones projecting a QR code in the sky? A 1,500-strong drone show created a scannable QR code in eastern China's Shanghai to celebrate the first anniversary of the Chinese release of the video game *Princess Connect!*

And, finally, Elimisha Kakuma is a college-preparatory gap-year program for Kakuma Refugee Camp refugees in northwestern Kenya, founded in 2021 by former refugees. The three founders studied in the United States at Harvard, George Washington University, and St. Olaf College!

As higher education becomes increasingly accessible to refugees, it will not only enhance their long-term life outcomes but also contribute to the overall strengthening of their communities.

So we live in an era of ideas. Nothing is too crazy or too "out there" to work.

That's not the way it's always been. Not that long ago, we lived in a world where limitations were well defined. Maybe people in the past had tried to test those parameters but had failed. And because people don't like failure, those mistakes became established constraints.

But today, we embrace failure. We even have a Museum of Failure.

The museum features a collection of failed products and services. Among them are the Apple Newton, a personal digital assistant; Bic for Her, a pen supposedly designed for women available in pink and purple; Google Glass, a brand of smart glasses; the N-Gage, a smartphone combining features of a mobile phone and a handheld game system; and Harley-Davidson perfume, which was largely a failed branding exercise.

While the 150 examples of failed products and services are funny to read about, the point is to destigmatize failure and recast it as a way to drive innovation. The founder of the museum says that its goal is to help people recognize that "we need to accept failure if we want to progress. Yes, it's okay to fail, but you have to learn something from the experience," he adds.[18]

In other words, *failure is good*. Failure is a process of figuring things out, and technology makes that possible.

And, as Jack Ma says, it's about being first—or at least understanding where the leading edge is and getting close to it.

4

WHEN DECIDING WHAT TO STUDY, THE KEY THING IS TO JUST DECIDE

If you're having a hard time deciding what to study in college, it may be helpful to think about the competitive TV show *Chopped* on the Food Network.

On the program, chefs need to whip up meals from a number of "mystery ingredients," which are often quirky and ill matched. Just before the competition begins, the chefs open a box and retrieve the foodstuffs they've been assigned one by one. An example of a past selection: rack of venison, seaweed, gooseberry preserves, and Froot Loops fruit-flavored cereal.

The chefs have only a few moments to ponder possible combinations before the announcer says, *Time starts now!*

And at that moment, a split second before scrambling into action—whizzing that cereal in a Cuisinart and using the resultant powder to coat the venison before roasting, melting the berry preserves with the seaweed to make a glaze—the chefs do something important.

They make a decision.

The prospect of making a decision can be overwhelming, particularly if the stakes are high and the options complex. Some of the chefs on *Chopped* are obviously at a loss as to how to use the mystery ingredients, and their inability to make a coherent decision becomes evident when they serve often unappetizing dishes to the show's judges.

At the same time, the process of deciding can be daunting. When dealing with these unorthodox food combinations, the probability of making something unpalatable—or, worse, inedible—feels high. When you are afraid of making a mistake, you can become nearly paralyzed by that fear. An irrational voice inside you is saying, *If you don't do anything, at least you won't make a fool of yourself.*

That's basically a fear of failure.

But let's say you contemplate going all out for the win and try something unexpected and borderline nuts—like making venison-flavored ice cream served with a Froot Loops and seaweed crumble. No one else could possibly think up such a wild combination of flavors.

There's a possibility that this kind of creativity and innovation might score you a win.

But what might keep you from executing your plan is a fear of success.

Sure, that seems counterintuitive. But some people feel anxiety or apprehension specifically related to attaining success and, potentially, their full potential. They don't want to try hard to achieve something because it brings increased expectations. That, in turn, stokes a fear of not being able to maintain that level of success.

So, by holding back or underperforming, one can avoid the pressure that success can bring. You can also avoid the humiliation that you envision could accompany crashing and burning from such a height.

You know, the higher they rise, the harder they fall.

When it comes to the college application process, you might be feeling either a fear of failure or a fear of success, maybe even a combination of both.

If it's a competition about getting into the "best" school, your feelings about participating can go either way.

No matter the reason, you might be tempted to not give it your best shot because you figure that no matter the effort you make, the outcome will be dissatisfying.

As a matter of fact, it might feel good telling your friends that you're not even trying because if you couldn't be bothered to rally to get into your "reach" school, you won't be embarrassed when you aren't accepted.

And maybe you feel like you don't deserve to get into a challenging program because you're just not smart enough.

There's nothing to be humiliated about when it comes to college applications. You have a tremendous amount to gain by going to college no matter where you go. It's a win-win situation. And the focus should be on getting into a challenging program that will serve your strengths rather than work against them.

If you think about it, one of the reasons why the college applications process has felt so stressful is due largely to the fact that, up until this point, it has felt so out of your control. By giving in to that feeling, you only make things worse.

As a matter of fact, it can feel empowering to finally take charge of a situation that has felt unnavigable and commit to making a choice.

When you decide to make a decision about what to study in college, you are taking that key step to making your college experience your own.

So congratulations on deciding to decide! That means you care about your education. It also means you trust your own judgment, which is also a big statement to make.

Recognizing the need to make a decision helps you focus your attention and resources on the problem or opportunity at hand. It enables you to clarify your goals and objectives, identify the options available to you, and evaluate the potential consequences of your choices. You don't need to get overly anxious about it. Any decision will give you direction and something to work from, and that's all you need.

It doesn't mean that you will necessarily end up at some particular goal, but it will give your life shape, which is better than falling through doors you didn't choose to open.

Because if you can't make a decision, the world will make one for you.

You can also involve others in the process to seek their input and perspectives. This could be your school counselor and your parents. This can lead to a more informed and inclusive decision.

But, in short, recognizing the need to decide is a crucial first step in any decision-making process, as it sets the stage for gathering information, analyzing options, and making an informed choice.

What you should also feel is excitement about the possibilities that lie ahead.

So let's get started!

Like the chefs on *Chopped*, you likely have several limitations to contend with. Hopefully, they aren't as disparate as combining Gummi Bears with filet mignon, but they are parameters nevertheless.

Often, however, restrictions lead to a creative solution and one that is better tailored to what you truly want and need.

Sometimes breaking down those limitations and translating them into actionable steps makes this formidable feat much more doable.

Let's start at the very beginning. Many people believe that they are either left-brained or right-brained. While this presumption is not scientific, it's a convenient shorthand to distinguish people with different personality traits and abilities. The concept behind this is a popular but oversimplified idea that people have dominant brain hemispheres that determine personality, thinking style, and behavior.

Along those lines, left-brained people are described as being logical, analytical, and orderly. So, based on that belief, left-brained students might pursue academic areas that require them to be logical and analytical. These can include math, science, and engineering.

In contrast, right-brained people are thought of as creative, intuitive, and good at art and music. They might be drawn toward studying a subject under the umbrella of the humanities, which encompasses English, history, art history, philosophy, and foreign languages, among other academic areas.

It's important to remember that we are really "all-brained." Just because you lean left or right doesn't mean you can't also embrace both sides of the three-pound organ positioned in your head that is basically keeping you alive. But everyone has unique strengths and weaknesses, so for purposes of your college decision making, you probably already know which category you instinctively fall into.

If you look at college majors overall, you can lump them generally into those that are for the left-brained and those that are for the right-brained. This will likely align with the classes that you either enjoy or do well in at school.

This could send you in several directions. Some colleges and universities are geared more toward math, science, and engineering, and others are known for their humanities and fine arts programs. Smaller private colleges, many of which are in the northeastern United States, are best known for their liberal arts programs, providing students with a broad-based, interdisciplinary education in the humanities, social sciences, and natural sciences. Big state universities tend to have a wide range of programs, and some are known for particularly highly regarded departments, like engineering at the University of Illinois Urbana-Champaign.

There are schools that, simply by their names, indicate what their strengths are. For example, Caltech specializes in science, engineering, and technology, as does the Georgia Institute of Technology.

Rensselaer Polytechnic Institute (RPI) is famous for the institution's ability to transfer technology from the laboratory to the marketplace. That's no surprise, as the word "polytechnic" refers to an institution of higher education offering courses in many subjects, especially those traditionally regarded as vocational or technical.

Similarly, the Parsons School of Design and Savannah College of Art and Design also wear their specialties on their sleeves. So, as you scan the horizon for university possibilities, whether you be left-brained or right-brained, you will likely come across these obvious choices.

However, you'll need to do a deeper dive to dig up the best programs in more subtle places. A good example is Carnegie Mellon University (CMU). CMU was established in 1967 with the merging of the Carnegie Institute of Technology and the Mellon Institute of Industrial Research, so it's not surprising that CMU has some of the most highly regarded engineering and computer science departments in the country.

But CMU's School of Drama is also one of the best in the country, usually uttered in the same breath as the Juilliard School and the Tisch School of the Arts at NYU.

The university's alumni have won 52 Tony awards to date[1] as well as 13 Academy Awards and at least 142 Emmy Awards (alumni and faculty). In fact, CMU has become the Tony Awards' first-ever partner from higher education.[2] They are teaming up to make a special program that will recognize and celebrate theater teachers working with students from kindergarten to high school.

The point is, don't go just by your first impression. Many universities offer a wide range of majors that are of very high quality, but you'll need to do a little delving to unearth them.

You may be taking a more brass-tacks approach to figuring out your major, left and right brains notwithstanding. And that approach might be studying a subject that will optimize your chances of clinching a well-paying job on graduation. Considering the cost of tuition, that's not a bad strategy for many. Fortunately, for those interested in securing a high salary on graduation, salary data are available that will guide you in the right direction.

One thing you'll quickly find, however, is that that salary compass will point you to one major and one major alone: engineering.

Eight of the top 10 majors with graduates earning the most money are subsets of engineering, according to a recent study by the New York Federal Reserve.[3]

Chemical engineering majors take the top spot, as graduates earn a median annual salary of $75,000 shortly after college. Some estimates indicate an even higher median annual salary of $105,550.

Chemical engineers apply the principles of chemistry, physics, biology, and mathematics to design and develop processes for the production, transformation, and use of materials and chemicals. They work in a variety of industries, including pharmaceuticals, energy, biotechnology, food, chemicals, and materials.

The importance of engineering to employers is evident in the Federal Reserve list—among the other top majors are computer engineering, aerospace engineering, and electrical engineering. Computer science and business analytics are the only two nonengineering majors that appear in the top 10.

Engineering is highly valued by employers because engineers possess the ability to transform ideas into reality, simulate and refine products through computer programming, and ensure the durability and safety of structures. In other words, you want to make sure that buildings don't collapse and that bridges don't fall down.

Engineers are needed in many industries, including computer technology, resource extraction, manufacturing, and construction. Engineering is a STEM occupation, and STEM jobs are expected to increase twice as fast as non-STEM jobs through 2031.[4]

Interested in universities where the graduates make the most money?

It's not surprising that several technical colleges are in that category. They generally specialize in vocational or job-specific training, especially in STEM fields, which, as we have just seen, are also the best-paying college majors.[5]

The *New York Times* used Department of Education data to rank the median income in 2020 of those who attended school 10 years prior—regardless of whether they graduated—and received federal aid.[6]

The top school, according to this ranking, was Caltech, with a median income 10 years after attendance of $112,166 and a median debt among graduates of $17,747.

Second on the list was MIT, with a median income of $111,222 after 10 years and a median debt among graduates of $13,418.

Then comes Harvey Mudd College and Bentley University. Keep in mind that there are no Ivy League schools mentioned on the list yet.

The first Ivy League university—the University of Pennsylvania—appears in fifth place, followed by CMU. At number seven is the Stevens

Institute of Technology, which is one of the oldest technological universities in the United States and was the first U.S. college solely dedicated to mechanical engineering. Even though it comes in seventh in terms of producing graduates who make the most money, *U.S. News & World Report* ranks Stevens 83rd in its ranking of "Best Universities."[7]

The point is that if you're using rankings, make sure the rankings are based on factors that matter to you.

For those of you curious about the majors that will get you the lowest salary, we're looking at theology and religion majors, who make about $36,000 per year within five years of graduation.[8] This is followed by graduates who studied social services, family and consumer sciences, psychology, leisure and hospitality, and the performing arts.

Sadly, the list is finished off by four majors related to education—early childhood education, elementary education, special education, and miscellaneous education, all earning $40,000 in yearly salary.

It's important to note here that these careers bring another kind of enrichment that is perhaps more meaningful than money. There's a lot to be said about teaching children and teenagers to open their minds to a world of learning that can set the course for the remainder of their lives. How many times have you seen a famous person on TV talk about how a teacher changed how they felt about themselves and their abilities?

For Lin-Manuel Miranda, the playwright who created the musical *Hamilton*, it was a music teacher in elementary school who wrote a song about Martin Luther King Jr. that inspired him.[9] Singer John Legend credits his English teacher with pushing him to earn a scholarship to the University of Pennsylvania as an English major, which was the start of his songwriting career.[10] And for actor Jon Hamm of *Mad Men* fame, teachers became parent-like figures to him after he had lost his mother at a young age and his father some years after.[11]

"I've had some of the greatest teachers in the world," Hamm said in an interview, "and I owe a huge portion of my existence to them."

The presence of teachers, he added, "can be the difference between, literally, life and death."

It's impossible to assign a financial value to a profession that provides that kind of experience.

You have to decide what is most important. As the saying goes, money can't buy you happiness, so it's not the only measure of success.

And the world would be a poorer place if everyone pursued financial gain above all else.

So far, we've been discussing largely what are considered "traditional" majors. A traditional major is a field of study that is commonly associated with a particular academic discipline, such as education, engineering, and religion. These majors typically require a certain set of core courses and electives that are specific to the discipline and often lead to a specific career path or graduate studies in the same field.

Conversely, there are also "nontraditional" majors. This label refers to fields of study that are not commonly associated with a particular academic discipline or that combine multiple disciplines in a unique way.

These include environmental studies, women's studies, digital media, and entrepreneurship. These majors may have more flexible curricula that allow students to tailor their coursework to their interests and career goals.

You may find that some majors can straddle both categories. Marketing, a very popular major, is a good example of that.

Generally, a marketing degree is considered a traditional major when it is part of a traditional undergraduate program offered by a college or university. That means that the program is designed to be completed in four years, with a set curriculum that includes courses in marketing, business, and related subjects.

The program may also include courses in accounting, finance, management, and economics. Examples of schools where marketing is offered as a traditional major include the Wharton School at the University of Pennsylvania, the Ross School of Business at the University of Michigan, the Kenan-Flagler Business School at the University of North Carolina at Chapel Hill, and the Stern School of Business at NYU.

In contrast, nontraditional marketing programs may be offered by online or for-profit institutions and may have a more flexible curricula or delivery formats. Southern New Hampshire University offers an online marketing program that covers areas such as digital and social media marketing. The University of Maryland Global Campus also has an online marketing program, as does Western Governors University.

It's worth noting that even if a marketing degree is considered a traditional major in some contexts, the field of marketing itself is constantly evolving. New marketing strategies and technologies are emerging around-the-clock. With generative AI playing a huge role in how content is created, marketing programs need to adapt and evolve to stay relevant.

Overall, marketing, as part of a communication studies or liberal arts program, can provide comprehensive insights into various facets of the field, including digital media strategies, brand development, and the intricacies of consumer behavior. Additionally, students may explore other relevant subjects, such as market research, advertising, and public relations, to acquire a well-rounded understanding of the marketing landscape.

There are many reasons why students pursue marketing as a field of study. Most major companies have large marketing departments that are responsible for the promotion of products, public relations, and branding. Because companies across a wide variety of industries need to compete for customers, marketing has become a field with a wide range of job opportunities.

Choosing the right program may not be simply a matter of assessing what salaries graduates earned when they leave campus.

According to one survey, the University of Wisconsin-Madison is the top university for a career in marketing, with fresh graduates earning an average of $73,245.67,[12] followed by the University of Pennsylvania, whose marketing graduates make an average $112,878 in their first year after graduation.

Wait a minute—if its graduates are making more money, why is the University of Pennsylvania ranked below the University of Wisconsin-Madison?

Several factors contribute to this, one being that the University of Wisconsin has one of the lowest average net costs for federal loan recipients, $17,234, factoring in fees, books, supplies, and the like. This compares with the University of Pennsylvania's $25,046. In addition, the University of Wisconsin has an admission rate of 57 percent, which compares with the University of Pennsylvania's extremely selective 9 percent.[13]

Returning to the *Chopped* TV show metaphor, there are other limitations you might need to work with as you combine these ingredients. Are you looking only at public universities in your state, where you'd get a relatively cheaper tuition bill?

Do you have the option of looking at public universities in other states? Those will likely be more expensive than the counterparts in your home state but less pricey than private universities.

And the list goes on. Maybe your limitations can make you feel kind of discouraged. Maybe you wish you could just take on college selection without the constrictions of money or geography.

But remember—you can have too much of a good thing.

There is, in fact, a case to be made against having too many options. American psychologist Barry Schwartz believes that the dramatic explosion of choice—from the zillions of customized drinks you can select at Starbucks to the endless types of clothes you can parse through on Amazon—actually creates anxiety in individuals.

"Freedom is good, we believe, the more the better," Schwartz writes.[14] "The more choice we have, the more freedom we have. And since the more freedom we have, the better off we are, the more choice we have, the better off we are."

Schwartz said that while these assumptions make sense, research demonstrates they aren't necessarily true.

"Though choice is good, there can be too much of a good thing," he said. "And when there is, it leads to paralysis, to bad decisions, to a loss of self-control, and to dissatisfaction with even good decisions."

He continued to say that while this research was not specifically focused on the experiences of college students, there could be connections between the amount of choice college students have and low college completion rates.

"There is no question that options for college students have exploded in recent years," Schwartz said. "Core requirements have diminished, the number of possible majors has increased, and the variety of paths through those majors has increased as well. What can we expect all this 'liberation' to produce?"

In essence, the fewer choices people have, Schwartz argues, the lower the probability of buyer's remorse—meaning that it's less likely you will regret the choice you made. If you can pick between only a sesame bagel and a plain one, no biggie. But if you can also have blueberry, egg, rainbow-swirl, Asiago cheese, French toast–flavored, or an "everything" bagel, the stakes rise.

An obsession with choice encourages people to look for reasons why they didn't choose the right thing.

Schwartz calls this phenomenon the "paradox of choice." He wrote a book about it.

"Smart institutions aiming to increase completion will offer students choice, to be sure. But the choice will be within well-defined limits, or constraints, so that the path to success is clearly marked," he said. "Paradoxically, the more opportunities we give students to do exactly what they want, the less likely they are to do anything at all."

So the next time you're fretting about all the things you can't study in college, think about Schwartz's theory. Maybe when it comes to deciding what to study, the more limitations you have, the better!

5

FOLLOW YOUR COMPETENCIES, NOT YOUR PASSION

Now let's take a bit of a different take on deciding what to study and examine the process from a more emotional perspective.

When deciding what to study in college and the direction you want to head after you graduate, the rule of thumb has been to let your passion be your guide. Find the thing that you love to do and run with it.

People have been thinking this way for a long time.

"Choose a job you love, and you will never have to work a day in your life," says Confucius, the fifth-century Chinese philosopher.[1]

"The most powerful weapon on earth is the human soul on fire," exults Ferdinand Foch, the 19th-century French general and military theorist.[2]

Today, voices from the wealthy and influential echo the same theme.

"If you're passionate about something, then it will definitely work out for you," says singer Ariana Grande.[3]

"Passion is energy," says Oprah Winfrey, media executive and talk show host. "Feel the power that comes from focusing on what excites you."[4]

And finally, wise words from Steve Jobs, an innovator who talked the talk and more than walked the walk: "The only way to do great work is to love what you do."[5]

So there's a lot to say about passion. And the people who have it and can convert that passion into fruitful and satisfying careers are truly the fortunate ones.

But recently, a cacophony of voices has been pushing back on what, up until now, seems to have been a pretty solid theory. What could possibly be wrong with pursuing what you love?

Apparently, a lot.

Is your dream to work in the fashion business?

Some estimate that the starting salary to work at New York City–based *Vogue* magazine is $36,632, or about $3,053 a month.[6] Recently on LinkedIn, there was a job posting for an "Assistant to the Editor-in-Chief-American Vogue and Global Chief Content Officer." The salary range for the full-time, entry-level position was $60,000 to $80,000 a year.[7]

At the same time, the median monthly rent for a Manhattan apartment in March 2023 was $4,175, up 12.8 percent from a year earlier,[8] while the average rent was $5,115.[9]

Prices may be skewed by the cost of luxury properties but, still, paying that kind of rent against that kind of salary probably would give even the most ardent fashionista pause.

Now raise your hand if your dream is to sell sponges.

Hello? Anyone? It's fair to assume that few, if any of you, would say that sponges would be your passion. But if you ask Aaron Krause, the founder of the cleaning product company Scrub Daddy, he'd probably sing the praises of sponges until the cows came home.

Krause says that his business originated in his undergraduate years at Syracuse University. And he didn't go to that school with a whole lot of intention.

"My father came into my room in 11th grade with a protractor and a map, and he put it on Philadelphia, drew a circle and . . . said, 'Anywhere in here, I pay for, and anywhere outside, you pay for' and Syracuse was on the very edge of that limit," Krause said in an interview.[10] "Instead of laying out on the beach in Miami, I bundled up and went to class every day."

While the entrepreneur had originally gone to college to study business, he took so many psychology classes that he couldn't graduate in four years with a business degree. Since his father wouldn't pay for an extra year, Krause completed college with a degree in psychology, which ended up not being a bad thing.

"It turns out there is a lot of psychology in business," he said.

Krause had experimented with foam buffing pads, which he became familiar with when spending his free time washing cars with friends to make extra money. He would later sell those pads to the auto industry. But he also discovered inadvertently that polymer sponges would soften and harden depending on the temperature of the water: When exposed to hot water, the sponges become softer and more pliable, making it easier to squeeze and clean surfaces. Conversely, when rinsed with cold water, the sponges become firmer, allowing for better scrubbing and removal of tough stains.

To make his sponges memorable, he designed them with distinctive smiley faces and gave his company the catchy name of "Scrub Daddy." The uniqueness—and usefulness—of his product is the reason why Krause's company was valued in 2019 by *CEO Magazine* at $170 million.[11] A charming and effective appearance on the TV show *Shark Tank* helped, too; in fact, his pitch resulted in one of the show's most successful products ever.

So the point of this story is not to stock up on cleaning products. The point is to understand that people can be successful in often mundane niche capacities that do not necessarily involve a glamorous or desirable career.

Another example is Sara Blakely, the founder of Spanx, a highly successful shapewear company. You're probably familiar with those super-supportive undergarments people wear beneath tight-fitting clothing that smooth out any bumps and ridges.

Or maybe you're not familiar with these because you're too young. But believe me, for many people out there, Spanx is a game changer when it comes to "body-con" confidence.

What you might not know is that Blakely's original passion was to become a lawyer. She had always dreamed of becoming a trial attorney like her father. She debated in high school and continued to do so in college, where she also studied legal communications.

When the time came for Blakely to take the LSAT, the standardized test required by many law schools for entry, she didn't do well at all. It was a big blow for her, but she didn't give up. She enrolled in an LSAT prep course, worked extremely hard, and took the test again—only to score even worse by one point.

It was a crushing disappointment for her.

So how did she respond to this defeat? Try to go to business school? Head to corporate America?

Nope. Not even close.

"In my mind, the universe was now telling me to drive to Disney World and audition for the role of Goofy," she said in an interview.[12] Come again?

"But [Disney World] only auditioned people for the character roles every once in a while," she continued, "so in the meantime I got a job at Epcot."

This just goes to show you that innovators truly think outside the box, even when under duress. And those creative plans sometimes don't work out. Blakely indeed auditioned to be Goofy but was told she was too short. Instead, they offered her a chipmunk role, but she didn't end up taking it.

According to Blakely, Disney had a policy that required employees to stay in their initial positions for a certain period before transferring. So she continued operating Epcot rides.

Eventually, she grew weary of working at Disney and decided to move back home to live with her mother. You can imagine what her mood was like at this point!

Blakely took a job at a local company selling fax machines door-to-door. On her first day, she was given four ZIP codes and told to sell without any leads or a potential customers list.

Every day, Blakely woke up early and spent the whole day cold-calling, which means trying to sell fax machines to total strangers. This is a lot harder to do than, say, selling boxes of Girl Scout cookies.

Most people slammed the door in her face or tore up her business card. She even had encounters with police who escorted her out of buildings.

But despite these challenges, Blakely continued to believe she could succeed.

"I would spend much of my free time trying to figure out what I really wanted out of life and what my strengths were," she said. "I knew I was good at selling and that I eventually wanted to be self-employed. I thought, instead of fax machines, I'd love to sell something that I created and actually care about."

Blakely had a revelation while getting ready for a party. She realized she didn't have the right undergarment to create a smooth look under white pants. So she cut the feet off a pair of pantyhose and used them as underwear. This allowed her to have the slimming effect of the pantyhose's "control top" while keeping her feet bare in sandals.

When she saw how good her figure looked, she realized this was the opportunity she had been waiting for. And, voilà, Spanx was born!

What was a stopgap attempt at creating an undergarment marked the beginning of a company producing a unique kind of body shapewear that is thin, comfortable, and invisible under clothes.

Little did Blakely know that her impromptu idea would grow into a company valued at more than $1 billion, based on recent news sources.

In March 2012, Blakely made history as the world's youngest self-made female billionaire, according to *Forbes* magazine. She was also recognized as one of *Time*'s "100 Most Influential People." Headquartered in Atlanta, Georgia, Spanx has opened retail shops across the United States and expanded its reach to more than 50 countries worldwide.

Blakely credits much of her success to her attorney father—her original inspiration—but not so much because of his profession. It was because he encouraged his children to fail.

In fact, her dad wanted his kids to be unafraid of failure because that would free them to be adventurous and to think big.

"His attitude taught me to define failure as not trying something I want to do," she said in an interview, "instead of not achieving the right outcome."

Her entrepreneurial journey showcased her ability to identify a problem, develop a solution, and build a successful business outside of her original passion for law. While there are plenty of people who dream of becoming fashion designers, it's unlikely there are many who aspire to fashion the garments women wear under their clothes.

Although, considering Blakely's well-publicized success, there are probably more aspiring undergarment designers now!

The examples of Krause and Blakely are evidence that successful entrepreneurship often involves pursuing opportunities outside of one's initial passions. They demonstrate the importance of recognizing market potential, being adaptable, and leveraging one's skills and expertise in different domains to achieve entrepreneurial success.

In other words, you can work at a cool magazine and barely make your rent, or you can discover a solution to problems that people are familiar with and, in the process, afford an even nicer place to live.

That's not to say that paying your dues in the magazine industry won't pay off one day.

It's just that they may well not. And, in a worst-case scenario, you might find yourself saddled with student debt from your college education while working in an industry where making low wages is common.

You don't want to look out onto the horizon and see only an endless series of debt-weighted months paying down what you owe.

Sure, there's a possibility you might be promoted to a high-level position and be awarded a better salary. But in a competitive world, it's often not only your abilities that are considered.

The fashion industry requires a creative flair, a comfort dealing with a wide variety of influential people, from editors and designers to publicists and celebrities. But for those workers on a lower rung of the ladder, it could mean less about schmoozing and more about performing duties for those previously mentioned groups, from doing coffee runs to making lunch reservations at restaurants and picking up a boss's dry-cleaning.

This was pretty apparent in *The Devil Wears Prada,* a movie (based on a book of the same name) that depicted what the life of someone working at a *Vogue*-like magazine is like. Of course, it's fiction, but you can't help but think the book is based on real-life experiences—after all, the author did work for a while at *Vogue* magazine.

You have to be prepared for these challenges and the possibility that things won't turn out as you had planned.

So, when trying to figure out what you'd like to pursue, consider both your passions and your competencies. Think about where and how they align, if they do at all.

And then think about what sort of careers can develop from them. Take that information into consideration as you search for colleges that are strong in these areas but that also make sense financially for your future.

With that in mind, let's expand a bit on the topic of writing.

Let's say your dream is to be novelist. You've always been good at writing, and you're happy to spend hours composing stories in high school. You fantasize about writing bestsellers in a cozy cabin in Vermont. Your enthusiasm is further stoked by the feedback from your English teachers throughout your four years of high school, all of whom encourage you to continue with the craft. Maybe one of them is even writing one of your recommendation letters for your college application.

Walk into any bookstore or library, and the sheer number of books lining the shelves—much less those available on Amazon—is enough evidence to indicate that, yes, a writing career can be done.

Or can it?

Launching a career as a novelist straight after college graduation—and being financially independent—is a difficult endeavor. Getting published is competitive and, as an unproven author, would likely require getting an agent and writing an entire manuscript.

And even getting published doesn't guarantee financial security. In 2020, 98 percent of the books publishers released sold fewer than 5,000 copies.[13]

So you have a few choices.

You might throw caution to the wind and decide to study writing in college. Full stop. And good for you for being committed!

Some of the most well-known programs are at Brown University, the University of Iowa, and Yale, followed by Cornell and Harvard.[14] If you do a little research, all those schools have produced celebrated writers. The fact that so many of the prestigious programs are at pricey, private universities might be an indication that the students who major in writing may not need to worry that much about money.

Or you can veer toward what might be described as a creative writing–adjacent major, such as journalism or communications. Studying journalism can lead you to that previously mentioned fashion magazine but also to a wide variety of media outlets, from online newspapers to newswires and broadcast. If you major in communications, that might place you well for jobs in public relations and publicity, and those will be in a wide variety of industries. Companies need employees who know how to communicate to the public about the work they do.

Or you can take your writing abilities—which are valuable—and apply them to a completely different major. Lawyers, for example, need to write persuasively and clearly for a lot of the work they do and employ critical thinking. While the law profession is quickly evolving due to technology (a lot of legal information is available free on the internet), there are many opportunities in the field.

You can see that if you cast a wider net when contemplating your strengths, abilities, and passion, maybe there's a path forward that's both comfortable and satisfying for you.

Meanwhile, it's interesting to hear examples of what tremendously successful entrepreneurs have to say about passion versus practicality.

Tech entrepreneur Mark Cuban, who owns the National Basketball Association's Dallas Mavericks and is worth around $5.1 billion according to *Forbes*,[15] believes the practical can trump a far-fetched dream.

"One of the great lies of life is 'follow your passions,'" Cuban said on the *Amazon Insights for Entrepreneurs* series.[16] "Everybody tells you, 'Follow your passion, follow your passion.'"

Cuban once wanted to be a sports star but realized that would be a tough goal to achieve. He advises doing what you're good at rather than what you dream of.

"When you look at where you put in your effort, that tends to be the things that you are good at," Cuban says. "And if you put in enough time, you tend to get really good at it."

Interestingly, Howard Schultz, best known as the visionary behind Starbucks, the global coffeehouse chain, once dreamed of becoming a professional athlete, too. Perhaps these types of aspirations are common among successful entrepreneurs because they are inherently competitive!

But, inspired by a trip to Italy, Schultz envisioned transforming Starbucks into a coffeehouse experience centered around quality coffee. His "passion" for creating a unique customer experience ultimately drove the growth of Starbucks into a global brand despite his initial interests being different.

Jeff Bezos[17] also made his fortune by developing a business based on an idea rather than by pursuing his passion, as burning as it was.

"Ever since I was five years old—that's when Neil Armstrong stepped onto the surface of the moon—I've been passionate about space, rockets, rocket engines, space travel," the Amazon founder says.

In a 2010 commencement address at his alma mater, Princeton University, he was also what he describes as a "garage inventor," meaning he took on projects in his family home's garage. Among his inventions were an automatic gate closer constructed from cement-filled tires, a solar cooker made from an umbrella and tinfoil, and baking pan alarms to entrap his siblings.

Later in his life, he discovered that Web usage was growing at 2,300 percent per year. He had never heard of anything that grew that fast, and the idea of building an online bookstore with millions of titles (something that didn't exist in the physical world) excited him—but in probably a different way than his passion for space.

And, as they say, the rest is history.

So, until now, the conventional wisdom has deemed college as a time to focus on what you love to do. And if you don't know what you love to do, you can spend that time figuring it out.

Sure, there was a time when students could go to college simply with the purpose to "find themselves." But that was when tuition was much cheaper.

In 1997–1998, around when your parents were in college, annual tuition and fees for a Californian student at UCLA were only around $4,050. Out-of-state students paid $13,034.[18]

In those days, students could afford to spend four years taking a bunch of random courses and playing Frisbee on the arts quad.

But today, in-state tuition at that same UCLA is $14,478, with out-of-state tuition a whopping $47,052. With that kind of cost, you don't have a minute to waste!

Sure, there are going to be people who will be unstoppable in their pursuits, driven by a force that defies logic or reason.

You're probably familiar with Greta Thunberg, the Swedish environmental activist who gained international attention for her efforts to combat climate change. Greta, now in her 20s, began her advocacy at age 15 to protest inaction on climate events, which sparked a global movement of student-led protests known as "Fridays for the Future." She's been nominated for a Nobel Peace Prize and named one of *Time* magazine's "100 Most Influential People."

Another prominent example is Malala Yousafzai, who, from a young age, was passionate about education and women's rights. Born in Pakistan in 1997, Malala was 11 years old when she began writing a blog for the BBC under a pseudonym, detailing her life under Taliban rule and advocating for girls' education. When she was 15, she was shot by the Taliban for her activism, but that didn't deter her. In 2014, she won the Nobel Peace Prize and became a global advocate for education, women's rights, and peace.

These individuals set a high bar in terms of what might be considered a passion. And if you feel strongly about a particular path, more power to you. But hopefully, for those of you who may still be finding a direction, incorporating an element of data and information can help you achieve success.

That's not to say you won't get there eventually. And if you feel like you don't really have a strong inclination, there's a lot to be said about simply forging a path. That path will lead you somewhere and give you focus, and you'll learn plenty along the way.

And if you find that something is more important to you later, you can change direction. But in the meantime, it's a good idea to align what you study with what you're good at—and, for good measure, what the job market needs. In other words, use your education to learn the skills employers are looking for.

Being employed and making a good salary will indeed make you feel good about yourself. And in certain subject areas, you can make that good feeling happen.

Technology, too, is a good area to explore. Above all, tech has disrupted the economy and all the industries within it. Technology and science jobs in the United States outnumbered qualified workers by roughly 3 million as of 2016. By 2030, there will be a global shortage of more than 85 million tech workers, representing $8.5 trillion in lost revenue.[19]

In other words, it's a matter of supply and demand. Even though companies are paying more to hire employees with the talent they need, there is still a shortage of high-skilled tech workers.

Plus, there are new jobs emerging all the time. Uber drivers, social media managers, podcast producers, UX designers, and cybersecurity specialists are all common jobs today that didn't exist in the past.

Indeed, the Bureau of Labor Statistics currently tracks employment in approximately 830[20] occupations, more than triple the 270 that were followed in 1950.

That means there are more jobs available for you, with even more possibilities likely in the future.

If having a secure job is your main goal on graduation, as we've discussed, a lot of data out there can help you make decisions about what to study to better your chances that that happens. If you make wise choices about how much the university you select charges in tuition and then balance that with what you want to do, there's no reason why you can't achieve your goal. And that accomplishment will eventually be fulfilling.

At this stage of the game, there's no reason why you'd graduate from college without a job or at least a pathway in the right direction.

If you love to read and want to write poetry, that's fine, too. In fact, it's great. We need poets, novelists, musicians, painters, and teachers—we especially need teachers.

But you don't need to spend $50,000 a year at an elite university to succeed at those things. Balance your goals against the cost and stress of getting into school.

At Google, an entry-level software engineer, most likely a recent college graduate, makes $193,902 in total compensation, according to one calculation.[21] Meanwhile, the estimated average salary for an entry-level reporter is $37,259.[22] That doesn't mean you shouldn't become a journalist. But it does mean you should consider spending less on your education to get there.

By the way, Bezos set aside his passion for space by building his e-commerce business. But in 2000, he founded Blue Origin, a privately funded company to enable commercial space travel and reduce the cost of access to space.

Bezos said in an interview, "I am currently liquidating about $1 billion a year of Amazon stock to fund Blue Origin. And I plan to continue to do that for a long time."[23] According to *Forbes*, Bezos is worth $143.3 billion and is currently the third-richest person in the world.[24]

In fact, Blue Origin landed a NASA contract for a Mars mission.[25] It is estimated that Bezos has so far invested at least $8 billion of his own money into this project, underscored by the entrepreneur's vision of millions of people living and working in space.

Bezos envisions tapping into the vast resources of space and enabling the movement of damaging industries away from Earth in an effort to preserve the planet.

"We're committed to building a road to space," the company's website reads, "so our children can build the future."

6

IN THE AGE OF TECH, THE HUMANITIES ARE MORE IMPORTANT THAN EVER

It may be counterintuitive to suggest that, in a world where screens are constantly demanding our attention and algorithms seem to govern our every move, the study of humanities has grown in importance.

That priority might seem improbable in your life right now.

Teenagers like you are logging up to 10 hours of screen time a day—via social media, gaming, online shopping, video chat, and texting—and that's in addition to sleeping, eating, and going to school.[1] How exactly you fit reading and writing and just thinking into that equation is unclear, but who's counting?

On a more macro level, technology largely dictates the course of major economies around the world. While in the past the size of a country's military determined its power, that weight has, at least in part, shifted to technological capacity. Battles continue to be fought on physical battle-fields, but an increasing number are waged in virtual fields, with hacking, state-sponsored cyberattacks, and online propaganda becoming weapons of choice.

This transition becomes apparent when you see the need for cyber-security experts continuing to outstrip supply. According to one estimate,[2] employer demand for cybersecurity workers grew 2.4 times more quickly than the overall rate across the U.S. economy. For approximately every 65 cybersecurity workers in the labor market—the majority already employed—there are 100 cybersecurity postings,[3] meaning there is more demand for those experts than there are experts to fill those spots.

"We can't accept leaving holes in our cybersecurity defenses simply because we don't have enough trained workers to plug them," said Will Markow, vice president of applied research at Lightcast, a company specializing in labor market analytics, in an interview.

But it is precisely because of the increasing influence of technology on everyday life that the importance of studying the humanities has been heightened.

In essence, the humanities are an attempt to understand what it means to be human! And the study of humanities helps us make sense of the world and our place in it by exploring the past, examining the present, and imagining the future.

President Barack Obama touted the importance of the humanities, especially with technology's increasing influence becoming more evident. By looking at what's happened before, students might be better equipped to contend with modern challenges.

"Throughout history, the arts and humanities have helped men and women around the globe grapple with the most challenging questions and come to know the most basic truths," he said.

The president added, "The arts play an important role in both shaping the character that defines us and reminding us of our shared humanity."[4]

If you are interested in literature, music, or fine arts, all the talk of jobs and data is noise. You see something that your peers do not. And that vision should be encouraged and carried through to your college education. Studying the humanities or liberal arts is inspirational and is for many continuing a tradition that reaches back through Walt Whitman to Shakespeare or John Cage to Vivaldi and beyond.

Should you be a playwright or a hedge fund manager? Even with the pauper-versus-prosperity comparison, for those interested in the humanities, the decision is obvious.

Sure, there's a lot to be said about pursuing STEM subjects. As a matter of fact, it's hard for that discussion not to monopolize everything right now. As discussed in earlier chapters, you really can't beat engineering and computer science if your priority is a high salary on graduation.

Plenty of data suggest that the job market is hungry for university graduates who have the skills to become software engineers and computer systems engineers. Considering how things are going, particularly with the rise of AI, this appetite is unlikely to decrease anytime soon.

This trend is occurring while the status of the liberal arts has started to lag.

Over the past 20 years, school counselors, school administrators, parents, and the media have convinced many young people to pursue STEM subjects. Or maybe young people have convinced themselves as they see an increasingly tech-forward world, influenced by Silicon Valley visionaries.

What about those literature and American history scholars? Not so much.

The number of college students graduating with a humanities major fell for the eighth straight year to fewer than 200,000 degrees in 2020, according to federal data.[5] Depending on how you define it, the drop in graduates is somewhere between 16 and 29 percent since 2012. The last time colleges produced so few humanities graduates was way back in 2002.

And it's not just about the numbers. When you look at the competition among academic departments for students, things look even bleaker.

In 2020, fewer than one in 10 college graduates were awarded humanities degrees. And get this—that includes majors like communications, which now makes up a quarter of all humanities graduates.

But if you narrow it down to traditional humanities like English, history, philosophy, and foreign languages, only 4 percent of college graduates in 2020 majored in these disciplines.

English language and literature—a major that used to account for a third of all humanities degrees—has been dealt a severe blow. In 2020, there were only about 37,000 college graduates who had majored in English, down roughly a third from 55,000 in 2009. History is also under pressure, down 25 percent.

That's a serious decline. People are worried about it.

And humanities aren't falling just because of interest in STEM. Majors in business and health-oriented fields are becoming more popular. In 2020, more than 430,000 college students graduated with business majors, up 60 percent in the past 20 years.[6]

And just for reference, engineering graduates more than doubled during the same period, with 195,000 students graduating in 2020, nearly matching the number of humanities graduates. And majors in health and medicine fields tripled in the past 20 years, with more than 260,000 graduates in 2020, way surpassing humanities majors.

So why are humanities taking such a hit?

There are several theories, a prominent one being rising tuition costs. If you spend a lot of money on a university education, you might want to—or feel obligated to—pursue more practical, career-oriented fields of study. After all, those student debts start accumulating as soon as you finish your degree, and it can take a while for humanities graduates to lock into a long-term career path.

But back in the 1990s, humanities majors were still on the rise, even when tuition and student debt were high. So there are probably other factors at play here.

Early college credits earned from AP courses and dual enrollment programs have allowed more students to skip humanities requirements. Even if you weren't particularly interested in humanities-type classes in high school, something might click at the college level. But if you've got large numbers of incoming freshmen placing out of introductory humanities classes, getting students to commit to humanities as a major becomes a challenge, as that environment is not allowing that "click" to happen.

Technology use and declining reading habits might also be impacting interest in the humanities. These subjects require a lot of reading in college, and with the rise in tech, students might be finding other interests.

But the stakes are high for academia, too. As humanities departments become less popular, they may have to hire fewer tenure-track professors and rely more on adjunct faculty. Those adjuncts are likely less experienced and qualified than professors and might not teach in the same compelling manner. This scenario can also further discourage students from pursuing humanities majors and create a downward spiral.

The signs ahead don't point to a turnaround, either.

Recent enrollment data[7] from the National Student Clearinghouse Research Center show that there were almost 9 percent fewer college students majoring in the liberal arts and humanities in the fall of 2021 compared to just two years earlier in 2019. English majors had seen a 10 percent decline in the spring of 2021 compared to 2020.

So that's the unadulterated bad news for the humanities. And, yes, there's a lot of it.

But there are reasons to believe humanities matter more than ever.

While technology plays a crucial role in shaping our world, it's important to remember that it is ultimately a tool. AI doesn't possess consciousness, much less a conscience (at least not yet!). All you need is a back-and-forth "discussion" with your friendly neighborhood AI bot to get a whiff of all the woolly issues associated with AI.

Those issues cover a wide range of topics, some of which you are likely becoming familiar with.

For example, deciding how much a student can utilize AI-generated text in assignments is something that schools and universities must contend with. What constitutes cheating and plagiarism is very different now than the word-for-word copying metric used in the past.

In addition, the "large language models" behind AI chatbots—computer programs that understand and generate human-like language—have been trained on vast amounts of text from the internet, meaning that the answers and information AI provides is based only on the text it has been trained on.

But if you consider all the English-language reading material in the world, it comes from some person's perspective, meaning that it's not neutral. And even if one person might consider the tone of an article to be neutral, another might consider it to be biased.

This could lead to the issue of bias in AI, as representation of a population's socioeconomic, cultural, and ethnic backgrounds may not be adequately reflected in the data that AI is being trained on.

So the ethical issues around AI—from plagiarism, ethics, bias, authenticity, misinformation, hallucinations (when an AI begins to spout false information), and privacy—are numerous. The list goes on and on.

But the discussion around how to best address these issues should probably come from sources more varied than just a group of engineers and computer scientists. They are all deeply invested in the advancement of technology and so may already be leaning in one direction before a dialogue can begin.

This is where the humanities come in; students studying humanities can explore the ethical implications of AI, the impact of social media on communication and relationships, or the ethical dilemmas associated with data privacy. Understanding the human side of technology can help young people develop a holistic view of its impact and make informed decisions about its use.

If you think about it, the examination of the influence of technology—from a non-tech perspective—could be both fascinating and helpful to society.

While technology has made our lives more convenient, it has also led to a decrease in face-to-face interactions and a potential decline in empathy and emotional intelligence. More profoundly, humanities help us understand our place in the world. From literature and art to history and philosophy, the humanities offer us a window into the experiences, beliefs, and values of people from different times and places.

That might sound a bit like some granola mumbo jumbo, but life is more than the nuts and bolts of tangible computers and mobile devices.

To truly understand the implications of tech and to be able to use it to its fullest potential, we need a deep understanding of human values, cultures, and perspectives.

And developing that understanding resides at the core of the humanities.

Don't think that the benefits of studying the humanities is limited to your contribution to society and the greater good. You can also personally benefit.

Studying the humanities will provide you with critical thinking skills, communication skills, and cultural literacy that are essential in a rapidly changing world. In a world dominated by technology, the ability to think critically is hugely important. The study of literature, history, and philosophy cultivates critical thinking skills by encouraging students to analyze and interpret complex information, consider multiple perspectives, and make reasoned judgments. It also gives you context, an important factor in understanding and contributing to the world.

These skills are crucial in navigating the vast amount of information available in the digital age and in making informed decisions about various issues that impact society.

Considering the rapid pace of change and the frequency of tech disruptions and the resultant challenges that arise with each iteration, these skills are more crucial than ever.

And these skills can be directly applied to the jobs you'll be looking at when you graduate from college.

The ability to think critically, to analyze complex issues, and to communicate effectively are skills that are highly valued by employers across industries. As technology and society advance, new skills will be required of our workforce. But employers are having a hard time finding university graduates with those skills.

In short, employers are now seeking skills that cannot be automated, such as communication, leadership, creativity, adaptability, and problem solving. With such a focus on producing graduates with degrees in engineering and math, our workforce is unprepared for this shift. In fact, three in four employers say they have a hard time finding graduates with the soft skills their companies need.

What exactly are those skills? Employees use critical thinking to analyze, evaluate, and reflect on information that they obtain through reading, communicating with others, and observing their environment. They then base judgments and decisions on this information. These could easily be the skills university graduates who studied the humanities or liberal arts could have acquired.

But a recent survey of 650 employers found that 64 percent of companies have difficulty finding qualified candidates with critical thinking skills.[8]

Meanwhile, communication skills are the most difficult to automate. Being able to communicate effectively entails listening, comprehension, reading body language, and relaying ideas in a clear, concise manner. While 77 percent of employers say communication is the most in-demand "human" skill,[9] more than half have difficulty finding potential candidates who possess it.[10]

So, as interest in STEM subjects rises, demand for university graduates with soft skills ideally will increase in tandem. The average company spends $800,000 looking for qualified candidates each year,[11] yet 60 percent of U.S. employers have job openings that remain unfilled for more than 12 weeks.[12]

In other words, humanities students of the world, unite!

Moreover, the humanities offer a unique perspective on the human experience that cannot be replicated by technology. They provide us with a deeper understanding of the world around us, the human condition, and the social and cultural factors that shape our lives.

Think about a book you've read that made you cry. Or after you finished the last page and closed the book's cover, you thought about the story for a long while. Or you listened to a piece of music that triggered a feeling inside you that was hard to describe.

That all could be part of your experience studying the humanities. And that experience can convert you to learning to write or compose those works of art that could move other people. You can imagine that the internal lives of students, writers, artists, and thinkers immersed in the humanities are quite different from those who are studying math and science. Think of it as the difference between a wooden kitchen chair and an overstuffed sofa. One is practical, but the other is comfortable. Which would you rather sit in?

This understanding is crucial for developing empathy, compassion, and a sense of social responsibility, all of which are essential for creating a more just and equitable society. In any population, you want people who are qualified to make the rules and those with the ability to analyze and question them.

Technology can be culturally homogenizing, while the humanities value diversity in cultures, traditions, and perspectives. Humanities can also encourage interests that, in the past, were not fully realized as credible areas of academic study.

This, in turn, fosters tolerance, acceptance, and inclusivity.

An example is a growing interest in studying identity. This is particularly important for a country that draws people from many different countries, ethnicities, and orientations.

There has been an increased focus on African American and Asian American studies in high schools. As you may have heard, the College Board offers an AP African American studies course,[13] and there is discussion of states mandating Asian American studies.[14]

For example, 26 U.S. colleges and universities now offer majors in Asian American studies, according to the College Board, and 72 universities offer relevant programs and resources, according to the Association for Asian American Studies. Those numbers continue to rise.[15]

With this type of orientation in high school, more students are likely to pursue related majors at university. And the career trajectories of graduates may also reflect this trend.

According to a LinkedIn research report, the hiring of chief diversity and inclusion officers has grown 168.9 percent since 2019.[16] While hiring for that role fell by 4.51 percent in 2022, it was the "C-suite" title (or roles with the word "chief" in it) with the fastest hiring growth in 2020 and 2021.

Part of that growth has been because many organizations have recognized that diversity can lead to improved results, including increased innovation and happier employees.

The humanities foster creativity by encouraging students to express themselves through writing and art and to explore new ideas and perspectives. Studying literature, for example, exposes you to different cultures and ideas, sparking your imagination. These skills are essential for adapting to the quickly evolving job market and finding innovative solutions to real-world problems.

The humanities play a crucial role in preserving and understanding one's cultural heritage. Literature, history, art, and philosophy are vital to understanding the values, beliefs, and traditions of different societies throughout history.

And a bit farther down the line, studying the humanities instills a love for learning and curiosity. To be valued in the workplace, you will likely need to develop new skills throughout your life, and humanities will empower you to continually seek knowledge.

Finally, you can develop a well-rounded and informed worldview that empowers you to navigate the challenges and opportunities of the modern world with wisdom, compassion, and resilience. By combining the benefits of technology with the insights of the humanities, we can create a future that is both technologically advanced and deeply human.

There's also some good news with regard to trends in the humanities.

A survey published in November 2021 shows that 90 percent of humanities graduates are generally satisfied with their lives and careers in 2019 even if their earnings, on average, slightly trail those of other majors ($58,000 versus $63,000).[17] More than 40 percent of humanities majors subsequently go on to graduate school, such as law school, for advanced degrees. Their earnings, then, are much higher.

It's worth noting that the same report mentions that 40 percent of humanities graduates say they would not choose the same major again. But that kind of buyer's remorse isn't uncommon when graduates are asked to look back on the academic decisions they made years ago regardless of major.

It's important to remember that the root of the word "humanities" comes from the Latin word *humanitas*, which means "human nature." The term was used by ancient Roman writers, such as Cicero and Seneca, to describe what makes humans distinct from other animals, such as reason, culture, and civilization.

In a time when social media feeds are filled with information and misinformation and online echo chambers can reinforce narrow perspectives, the humanities foster critical thinking skills. They teach us to question, analyze, and evaluate. They encourage us to seek multiple viewpoints, consider ethical implications, and think critically about the impact of technology on society.

So, even with what might seem like good reasons to pursue other subjects, don't hesitate to gravitate toward the humanities if that's where you feel you should go. To study what it means to be alive will be well worth it.

7

BUYING AN EDUCATION SHOULD BE LIKE BUYING A CELL PHONE

So your parents have decided to buy you a cell phone. *Yeah!*

Excited, you launch into detailed research about which make and model to pick, and this usually means an iPhone versus a Samsung. There seems to be an unwritten rule that when your parents buy you a phone, you shouldn't base your decision on personal whim. You feel obligated to compare your options, head-to-head, to make an informed decision.

Maybe it would be worth preparing a PowerPoint presentation to plead your case!

So let's take a look at your choices.

At first glance, an iPhone might feel pricey, with Samsung phones being considerably less expensive: one point for Samsung.

But iPhones have software that integrates with other Apple products, like AirPods and Apple watches: that's a check in the iPhone column. On the other hand, Samsung phones are generally cheaper to fix. But at the same time, some say that Samsungs lose their value more quickly, while iPhones can be easily traded in when it's time to upgrade.

And considering how often new iPhone versions are released, you want to be able to easily upgrade!

There's the issue of cameras, too. If you start comparing cameras, then we're wading into entirely new territory.

You understand the back-and-forth when checking out options. In fact, you've probably conducted the same type of due diligence when buying your own phone. And, yes, the money your parents could spend on your phone is considerable, and prices can vary—Samsung may have more lower-cost options, but their high-end models can cost more than an iPhone. Bravo for respecting your parents' hard-earned money! And if it's your own hard-earned money, bravo to you!

Now forget about the cell phone.

Your parents have decided to buy you a university education.

Comparison shopping for a university education and a cell phone may seem like very different activities, but there are several similarities between the two.

In both cases, you are looking for a product that meets your specific needs and preferences while being cost effective and providing the best possible value. And spending the time and thought in selecting your university should be a priority for you.

The reasons for that are obvious.

The average cost of college in the United States is $36,436 per student per year, including books, supplies, and daily living expenses.[1] That's like buying 40 iPhones! This cumulative sum has more than doubled in the 21st century.

Let's split that into state schools and private schools. The average in-state student attending a public four-year institution spends $26,027 for one academic year, $9,678 of which is tuition alone. Out-of-state tuition averages $27,091.

What's striking is that the average total a student pays per academic year when attending a private, nonprofit university is $55,840, with $38,768 of it on tuition and fees. Considering student loan interest and loss of income, the ultimate cost of a private university bachelor's degree can exceed $500,000.[2]

So put your phone down and let's start talking about what you need to do.

When shopping for a cell phone, you consider factors like features, performance, and price. Similarly, when comparing universities, students must evaluate the academic programs, facilities, reputation, location, and cost. In both cases, since you can't have everything you want, you need to prioritize needs and preferences to find the product that best suits your requirements.

You can consult with friends, family, or online reviews to gather more information and opinions about the universities you are considering. Like with a phone, you can read online reviews or watch "day in the life" videos of that university's students on YouTube. It might even be a good idea to contact alumni for an honest assessment about their experience.

But why are you less inclined to spend time researching universities the way you do phones?

When buying a phone, you might spend hours doing your research. When comparing universities, you may spend months or even years researching different institutions, attending college fairs, and talking to admissions officers to gather as much information as possible before making a final decision.

In addition, you might be more inclined to research cell phones because their use is more immediate and relevant. Finding the best value directly impacts your current needs and lifestyle. It's easier to think about buying phones because they are a common part of everyday life.

Moreover, planning to buy a phone is *fun*. You probably don't feel the same way about your university education.

But what if we look at "buying" your education in the same way you would an iPhone?

First, you'd go by price. Students should be doing some comparison shopping with regard to tuition and figuring out why some universities charge a premium and whether that extra charge is worth it. Some universities, particularly private ones, charge high tuition because of their well-known brand name.

Undoubtedly, some names simply open doors. That's the hard truth—while the value of brand is declining due to the importance of skills in the job market, there are still universities that resonate. Think about how you feel when you hear the words Amazon, Starbucks, Nike, and Tesla. You may or may not like those companies or their products, but you have a reaction.

People also have emotional reactions to certain university brands, and that's why so many students still clamor toward a few elite schools.

While ranking the most expensive universities varies depending on who's doing the ranking, it might be worth doing some horizon scanning to pluck the low-hanging (or, rather, high-reaching) fruit. Recently, Amherst College charged $66,650 in yearly tuition,[3] Harvey Mudd College $65,954,[4] and Columbia University $65,524.[5]

As eye-popping as those figures might be, these might be looked on as bargains when peering into the future. Based on annual college cost growth rates, a 2019 *Hechinger Report* projected that the University of Chicago would be the first U.S. university to cost $100,000 a year.[6] According to some estimates, the cost of living in Chicago is 19 percent higher than the national average,[7] so when we're talking about the "all-in" cost of going to school there, it's likely out of reach for most people.

But, like an iPhone versus a less expensive phone, sometimes a product's features make the price tag worth it. Or some people like being seen with a particular model just because they feel like it says something about who they are.

It's the same rationale as to why some people spend more than $900 for a men's designer T-shirt rather than $13 for one from Hanes. Both shirts serve the same function, yet there's something more than a person's wealth that draws a buyer to the pricier option.

Brand is pretty powerful. Some people believe that being associated with a particular brand, be it a T-shirt, a cell phone, or a university, says something about who they are. And it goes beyond functionality. Being associated with a famous brand can enhance an individual's social status, credibility, and perceived quality.

Think about how a character's wealth or status is portrayed in a movie. What do you think about a character that drives a fancy sports car, wears designer clothes, and lives in a famous neighborhood known for expensive mansions and groomed lawns? Visually, brand implies a lot.

With regard to a university, the same associations can apply. There's an appeal to being affiliated with a prestigious school, as people might conclude something about a student going there based on that—perhaps having to do with intelligence, ability, or ambition. And brand also provides a sense of belonging and prestige—think about all the swag and sweatshirts that alumni wear at football games, reunions, and even the gym.

But, like cell phones, what happens when you graduate and decide to "trade in" your diploma for a job? What kind of value does your education provide then?

It's worth investigating what kinds of relationships the universities you are looking at have with employers and if the jobs being offered are those you'd like to have. There may not be an obvious way to do this, although a university's locale and the companies based nearby could serve as a jumping-off point.

For example, the University of Oregon has a long relationship with Nike and the firm's cofounder Phil Knight. In fact, the University of Oregon has embraced a "University of Nike" image, and Knight has donated more than $1 billion to the university since the late 1980s.[8]

By the same token, Portland State University, close to the Nike Beaverton campus, has a logo that is an output of a partnership with Nike.[9] The company also has been known to recruit employees from their local university. So, if your dream is to work at an athletic apparel company, you may not need to go to a particularly fancy university.

In fact, employers have been known to shy away from long-distance hires in favor of local options.[10] The reasons are numerous, including the availability of local candidates for in-person interviews, minimal relocation costs (if any), and the absence of cultural adjustments for the new employee when getting acclimated to a new town or city. For more senior jobs, a company will recruit nationally, maybe even internationally. But for an entry-level job, if you're within in-person interview distance, you may already have an edge.

Sometimes the more niche your area of study or the more specialized your university, the greater the potential for unique partnerships. For example, Embry-Riddle Aeronautical University is a private university specializing in aviation and aerospace education with two main campuses: one in Daytona Beach, Florida, and the other in Prescott, Arizona.

Due to its unique specialization, Embry-Riddle partners with NASA, the Federal Aviation Administration, and large aerospace, security, and defense companies, including Diamond Aircraft.[11] The university builds strong relationships like these to provide essential learning opportunities for students and is strategically located only about 50 miles from the Kennedy Space Center.

As a result, Embry-Riddle has a large network of alumni in these industries, ranging from high military officials, airline business leaders, and intelligence agency officials. This is alongside NASA and Canadian Space Agency astronauts.

And don't be embarrassed if you decide you don't want to be too far from home.

Home is nice! And even though many high schoolers claim they want to get the heck out of Dodge when they graduate, 56 percent of first-time, full-time freshmen pick schools that are 100 miles or less from home, according to a 2019 survey by UCLA.[12]

Some estimate that as many as 85 percent of university students are defined as "commuter students," meaning they don't live in institution-owned housing on campus.[13] That includes students who, after a year or so of living in housing on campus, decide to move to apartments with friends.

Also, if you decide to go to a community college near home for a couple of years, your chances of getting into a named university may be better than if you had applied for a freshman place. For example, 95 percent of transfer students accepted to UC Berkeley came from California community colleges, and the admittance rate was around 26 percent.

In fact, almost a third of UC students are transfers, and almost all have come from community colleges.[14] A priority on having a diverse student population could be one of the reasons why transfer students are a focus.

That compares with a recent freshman admittance rate of 11 percent for the fall of 2022.[15] This so-called 2 + 2 model not only betters your chances of getting into a competitive school but also saves you money, as tuition at community colleges in California and many other states is generally inexpensive.

Getting back to the mobile phone. Let's say that despite any difference in trade-in value, you still want to go for that expensive model. What happens if you realize the phone doesn't really work as well as advertised?

For example, some of the world's best-known universities boast about the quality of the faculty but aren't transparent as to whether those professors are actually teaching or are delegating that task to graduate students.

In fact, in some cases, your chances of being taught by a professor may be better if you go to a lower-ranked college or university rather than a more branded one. The reasons for this are numerous, but a major one is that professors often prioritize research over teaching, so, if allowed, they delegate those pesky responsibilities to their students.

And sometimes those students are *undergraduates*.

For example, according to a 2013 article in the *Harvard Political Review*, Harvard University's statistics department hired 32 undergraduates (and 32 graduate students) to help teach courses over a semester.[16]

At Cornell, you might have gotten a renowned (and now retired) professor like James Maas teaching Psychology 101, but he addressed 1,600 students at one time. Back in 2000, the *New York Times* said, "It hardly sounds like a class that an Ivy League university charging nearly $25,000 a year in tuition would boast about."[17]

But what about at Cornell's $65,204 annual tuition price tag in 2023–2024?[18]

Fewer professors are teaching their classes.[19] Between 1988 and 2004, teaching loads for professors at research universities plummeted by 42 percent.[20] There may have been a number of reasons for that fall, but that still means less faculty engagement with students.

Even at liberal arts colleges, which pride themselves on their teaching, the time that professors spend in the classroom has fallen 32 percent[21] with TAs and graduate students picking up the slack.

Why the decline? With a reduced teaching load, professors have more time to conduct research, which can benefit both their personal careers and their employers. While research can often benefit the greater good—think of how universities helped with vaccine development to fight COVID-19—there are also financial advantages to consider.

Teaching a bunch of undergraduates Psychology 101 or holding office hours? This is definitely a plus for students but perhaps not as much for a professor's (or a university's) bottom line.

So, if you're largely not being taught by a university's renowned faculty, does it really matter what your school is ranked?

You may be the type of person for whom large classes are not a challenge. You are motivated enough to regularly seek out professors after lectures to develop personal connections.

If that's the case, kudos to you. That degree of maturity and resourcefulness will serve you well, even beyond higher education. But if you get lost in a crowd or could use a little guidance to help you along, going only by brand when it comes to a university may not be your best option.[22]

Being a stellar student at a lower-ranked school rather than in the middle of the pack or lower on the totem pole at a more selective university might mean more opportunities. Perhaps you'll have a better chance of being awarded a merit scholarship at a less competitive school if you're stronger academically than your peers. Professors might mentor you, too, as they are seeking excellent, resourceful students. You might even have a better chance of graduating on time.

Keep in mind that just because you go to college doesn't mean you're going to learn the right stuff. Employer surveys indicate that more than half of hiring managers think recent college graduates lack key competencies, such as oral and written communication.[23]

So, for those students who need more personal attention in acquiring competencies, a small, less renowned college where potentially more professors teach classes could be a better—and cheaper—fit.

Think of a freshman class in political science where a professor takes the time to critique the PowerPoint presentation you and your assigned group put together on the differences between a nation and a state. The professor would let you know if your points were clearly made and supported and if the ideas put forth were fresh and original.

This kind of personal attention could help you improve your communication and critical thinking skills and build your team's ability to work together—all competencies that employers are looking for.

In fact, *U.S. News and World Report* ranks the country's colleges and universities that focus on undergraduate teaching rather than on conducting research. Certainly, there are Ivy League universities on the list, but Elon University in Elon, North Carolina, ranks number 1! That school is followed by Brown and Princeton, then Rice University and Boston College. The University of Maryland Baltimore County, Gonzaga University, and Marquette University all beat out Harvard on this ranking, which comes in at number 18.[24]

It's worth figuring out exactly what you want to get out of your classes and which schools suit your academic and financial needs.

In fact, research conducted by Georgetown University's Center on Education and the Workforce finds that a good number of college graduates *are* showing buyer's remorse.[25] If given the chance, more than half would have gone to a different college or chosen a different major.

Further, a Gallup-Purdue University study of university graduates shows that a transformative college experience is linked more closely to satisfactory professional outcomes than to a university's ranking.[26]

The study found that the type of school that college graduates attended—public or private, small or large, or very selective or less so—hardly related to their workplace engagement and current well-being.

Instead, the support and experiences a student had in college had a much greater impact on long-term outcomes for these graduates. If a graduate had a professor who cared about them as a person, excited them about learning, and encouraged them in their pursuits, their odds of being engaged at work more than doubled, as did their odds of thriving in all aspects of their well-being.

Yet only 3 percent of all the graduates examined for this research had these types of enriching college experiences. And it's unlikely that the graduates making up that 3 percent came only from selective universities.

If graduates had an internship or job in college, were actively involved in extracurricular activities and organizations, or worked on projects that took a semester or more to complete, their odds of being engaged at work doubled as well.

So, if you find a school that can provide you with these opportunities, you'll better your chances of graduating to happiness.

The stakes couldn't be higher. According to a report from the Georgetown University Center on Education and the Workforce, between 1980 and 2020, the average cost of tuition, fees, and room and board for an undergraduate degree rose 169 percent.[27]

Students and families want—and need—to know the value they are getting for their investment. Going to college has become one of the biggest investments people make in their lives.

College can provide large rewards, with graduates earning more than $1 million more on average over a lifetime than high school graduates.[28] But going to college without thinking through what you will study also involves substantial risk, with a $3.4 million difference in lifetime earnings between the highest- and lowest-paying majors.[29]

That's not to say that salary is the most important driver in making your college decisions. For many, it isn't, and it shouldn't be. The point is to be informed.

In the world of consumer electronics, a new phone may be the latest and greatest for a few months, maybe a year if you're lucky. But investing in a university education can provide benefits that last a lifetime.

So the next time you're upgrading your phone, ask yourself, *How much time should I spend investing in something that will truly stand the test of time?*

8

IF YOU'RE SET ON HARVARD, TRY THE ONE IN JAPAN

For many people, attending an Ivy League school isn't a possibility. It almost feels like there's not much room to get any more exclusive unless they stop accepting new students altogether! But fortunately, if experiencing what it's like to get an elite education is something you really want, there are ways to do that without trying to squeak in with record-low acceptance rates.

What if you went to the Harvard of Japan?

The University of Tokyo is the most prestigious university in Japan and at one point was the most highly regarded university in Asia. With strengths in engineering, physics, and materials science, the university offers a high-quality education that could rival that of Ivy League schools. And it charges less than a tenth of what Ivy League universities do, with yearly tuition just below $4,000, based on current exchange rates.

Of course, it's impossible to draw an equivalence between one university in a given country and one in a different country. There are huge distinctions in education systems, historical factors, and funding. But the point is that you can explore the possibility of going to the most highly ranked university overseas.

In Denmark, that would probably be the University of Copenhagen. In China, that would be either Tsinghua University or Beijing University, while in Korea, it's Seoul National University. In Canada, people will likely say either the University of Toronto or McGill University. Of course, there will be opinions about other universities that might be considered the most prestigious. But the point is that there are elite institutions across the globe.

You're probably aware of the best-known universities in the United Kingdom—Oxford University and Cambridge University. In fact, those two are so sought after that people often combine the two names and refer to them as a single entity: Oxbridge.

While it is still very competitive to get into Oxford, for example, the admissions rate is significantly higher than for some of the Ivy League options in the United States.[1] Tuition depends on your course of study, with yearly fees range from $36,122 to $54,900. And even if you end up on the high end of that scale, in the United Kingdom you earn a degree in three years!

In Scotland, a university education takes four years, but tuition fees there tend to be lower. For example, a year at the University of Edinburgh costs $27,456.

And that's even considering the fact that tuition is usually considerably more expensive for non-U.K. students than for U.K. students. The system is similar to how in-state students in the United States can pay significantly less at their flagship public universities than the students who come from out of state. For example, if you were from New York, you'd pay less to attend the State University of New York at Purchase than a student who is from New Jersey.

You may also find that living expenses in some countries may be lower than in the United States, which can also help make studying abroad more affordable. According to the World Economic Forum, New York, San Francisco, and Los Angeles—where many popular U.S. universities are located—are among the top 10 most expensive cities in the world. In contrast, Osaka and Tokyo, Japan; Manchester, United Kingdom; and Busan, South Korea—all cities that host major, competitive universities—are among the top 10 cities in the world where living costs are falling.[2]

Some students in the United States might not know that many universities in non–English-speaking countries have curricula that are taught in English. Those universities adopt English as a medium of instruction, employing the English language to deliver their academic curricula. This enables students from diverse backgrounds to study there even if they don't speak the local language.

So where you might go to study doesn't necessarily depend on your ability to speak a foreign language. But no matter where you go, studying overseas will give you a tremendous opportunity to learn a language that is native to the people around you. Whether it be Japanese, French, or Korean, learning a language will only serve you well while you are living overseas or when you return home to start looking for a job.

In addition, studying at a university overseas can be a great way to broaden your horizons and gain a different perspective on your field of study (if not on the world). It can also be a chance to experience a different culture, which can be an enriching experience in itself. You would be socializing with students from other countries, understanding local customs, and even figuring out how to use the subway system—learning isn't limited to the classroom.

One of the most enjoyable things to do when in a foreign country is to go to the local grocery store. It's fascinating to see what people are buying in terms of everyday items, such as milk, bread, cookies, and crackers. Often what you see, too, reflects something about the country you are in.

Take the cookie aisle—excuse me, I mean the "biscuit" aisle—at a supermarket in London. Strolling by those boxes of Jaffa Cakes, Jammy Dodgers, and HobNobs, you might see how Britain's past and the custom of afternoon tea influence British snack preferences.

Have you ever been to the regular cheese section at a French supermarket? You'll be astonished at the variety and quantity of what the ordinary French consumer expects. You'll also be able to better understand how France, which according to some estimates produces 1,000 different types of cheese,[3] values its signature delicacy.

Additionally, studying abroad can help students develop valuable skills, such as independence, adaptability, and cross-cultural communication, which can be highly valued by employers.

Students who are thinking about studying overseas often don't think about how that experience can benefit them both personally and professionally.

Being overseas can make you aware of the fact that there's more than one way to do something. Take a subway in New York City and then take one in Seoul, Tokyo, or London. You'll see that public transportation is run in very different ways around the world.

What might be considered a simple task in the United States—like opening a bank account or mailing a package at the post office—can be a complex undertaking in another country. But by overcoming these hurdles, you can get a huge sense of accomplishment.

In addition, you might also gain a new appreciation for the way things are done back home!

There are scholarships to help cover the cost of studying abroad, and you can also use financial aid to fund this pursuit. While figuring out the finances for study abroad can be taxing, it will be well worth your efforts.

A number of famous people have studied abroad at both undergraduate and graduate levels. While many of them did not complete an entire degree abroad, their experiences have been undoubtedly formative.

Among them are actors Julie Bowen (Italy) and Gwyneth Paltrow (Spain), designer Vera Wang (France), singer/actor Darren Criss (Italy), LinkedIn founder Reid Hoffman (United Kingdom), Food Network chef Alton Brown (Italy), and former president Bill Clinton (United Kingdom). Back then, options to study a full undergraduate degree abroad were more limited than they are today.

But things have changed. You may have read that actor Angelina Jolie's oldest child, Maddox, became a full-time student at Yonsei University in Seoul.

And what you get out of your education doesn't need to necessarily correlate with what you end up doing.

Caroline Schiff, the executive pastry chef at Brooklyn's famous Gage & Tollner restaurant, received a degree in French from the University of St. Andrews in Scotland. That school might sound familiar because that's also where Prince William went to college.

Back then, Schiff wasn't necessarily drawn to the culinary arts. "I didn't know what path my career would take at the time, but I figured a [liberal arts] degree would be useful," she said.[4]

But while doing an "abroad abroad" program at the Université de Grenoble in France while a student at St. Andrews, Schiff would walk to class and pass a small chocolate shop that carried hand-dipped chocolates and constructed Eiffel Tower chocolate sculptures. "It was clear to me that this was art," she said.

So studying abroad can open doors, not necessarily directly to jobs but in your mind.

However, if you still insist on getting a taste of Harvard, MIT, or other branded schools, your wish can be fulfilled. Even if you don't have the grades or money to attend "that school in Boston," there are many ways to get an elite education.

EdX is the massive open online course (MOOC) provider created by Harvard and MIT. It offers courses from some of the world's top universities, including Harvard, MIT, and Columbia. This gives students the opportunity to learn from some of the most respected scholars in their fields.

The online platform offers courses in a wide range of disciplines, with Harvard providing around 140 free courses. You can choose to receive a certificate for a small fee, making these courses a more accessible option for students who might not otherwise be able to attend top-tier schools.

One of the more popular courses is "CS50," Harvard's Introduction to Computer Science course. The lecture course is delivered live to around 800 students in an auditorium on the Harvard campus and streamed free of charge as "CS50x" to thousands of students across the globe, eager for a taste of what a Harvard class is like.

A good example of the potential of the class took place in the spring of 2021.

On April 23 of that year, Harvard University computer science professor Dr. David J. Malan tweeted a photo of himself after getting vaccinated against COVID-19 at a Walmart. Like many, he had made an appointment using the superstore's online vaccination booking system.

Shortly after his tweet went out, Malan received a message[5] from Anirudh Konduru, a recent graduate from a college in Bangalore, India: "Hey David! Noticed you got your vaccine at Walmart. Thought you'd be interested to know that the guy who wrote a significant part of the back-end code that handles Walmart's online vaccine bookings, yours truly, first learned how to code years ago from you, from CS50x. Thank you."

CS50x has gained a cultlike following since Malan started teaching it in 2007. While many of the students who sign up for the online CS50x—more than 4 million to date—eventually drop out, the payoff for those like Anirudh who muscle through and complete all the assignments can be nothing short of life changing.

So we're talking about the power of access.

When massive open online classes were introduced in 2008, they were viewed as game changers, democratizing education and giving opportunities to students globally regardless of academic records or financial resources. Dropping out, of course, was and remains a problem.

Even for the highly produced, cinematic CS50x, the same drop-out rate prevails—out of the 150,349 students who registered for the class in 2013, for example, only 1,388 received certificates. Students like Anirudh are the exception rather than the rule.

Anirudh, who became a software development engineer for Walmart Labs based in Bangalore after college, took CS50x when he was a high school senior. Uncertain about what he wanted to study in college (he was toying with a medical career), he felt that developing a basic knowledge of computer science would be a good idea.

While he was initially drawn to CS50x due to the Harvard brand, the usefulness of what was taught compelled him to finish the course even as he graduated from high school and began college.

"The Harvard name helped legitimize the course, but once you start the class and do a week or two, it's the content that matters," Anirudh said.

After finishing CS50x, Anirudh decided to major in computer science, graduating from R.V. College of Engineering in Bangalore in 2019 and then joining Walmart Labs. In June 2020, he began working on a team to develop Walmart's vaccination reservation system, which launched in August that same year, initially for the distribution of regular flu vaccines and then later for those that protect against the coronavirus.

While noting that many students in countries like India are unable to benefit from free online classes because they lack access to computers and the internet, Anirudh encourages his peers with resources to try out some free Harvard classes.

"This course helps build passion, especially when you go that extra mile to learn on your own," said Anirudh, who has since graduated with a master's degree in computer and information science from the University of Pennsylvania and moved to Seattle, Washington, for a software engineering job. "It definitely gets you into the field."

Online education is nibbling away at the proprietary nature of what an Ivy League school offers its students. While the initial excitement prompted by the widespread adoption of MOOCs has since been mitigated by high drop-out rates, as mentioned earlier, the wide availability of quality online courses for students who are mature and self-motivated enough to complete them is a game changer.

In addition, the ability for elite universities to engage with students who are economically disadvantaged will also change how they view their roles in serving the greater societal good.

In other words, how many millions of Anirudhs are out there, their lives changed because of a free online class they have taken?

And for those who want to be a part of Harvard no matter what, there's the Harvard Extension School. You simply need a minimum 3.0 GPA[6] for a degree program and a desire to be part of the school's community. While the school's offerings are designed for people who have worked for a number of years, graduates of degree programs become full-fledged members of the Harvard alumni network and can attend social events and use university clubs and resources.

The network you could develop would also be substantive, as graduates are more likely to be working professionals.

So, to put it simply, there are many ways to get a taste of what might be considered an elite education. But the most important thing, no matter what path you choose, is to work hard, stay motivated, and make the most of what you have.

You can achieve your goals and pursue your dreams no matter where you go to school!

9

IT'S NOT THE GRADES YOU MAKE, IT'S THE HANDS YOU SHAKE!

It's never too early to start thinking about networking, even if getting a job feels like it's in the distant future. At UCLA, freshmen are advised to visit the university career center within their first year.

In fact, you've probably been networking your whole life without realizing it, and you're likely pretty good at it!

You landed a babysitting job because you found out through your parents that a family needed help with their child. Or you got a solid recommendation letter from your favorite English teacher because you had developed a great relationship with them. Or maybe you were elected president of your high school's yearbook club because you were able to convince fellow students you were the right person for the job.

All these opportunities were made possible by your ability to network.

Or maybe you aren't that kind of student. Maybe you aren't one to participate in high school activities and generally like to keep to yourself. Don't worry—networking is something you can pick up at any time!

But as you're making decisions about college, it's a good idea to start dipping your toes into the networking pool. So, let's first define what networking means.

For many, the term leaves a bad taste in their mouths. It can feel transactional, like an "I'll scratch your back if you scratch mine" kind of arrangement that doesn't sit right with you. We've all seen videos of chimpanzees grooming each other's fur.

But there's nothing unseemly about it. It's the way the world works, and the earlier you understand that, the better off you'll be. There is also the old adage, "It's not what you know, it's who you know." That means that knowing the right people can sometimes be more important than what you are able to do.

In the past, it was believed that students who attended prestigious universities had better opportunities to get to know the right people. It was based on the idea of an "old boys' network" where opportunities were communicated through word of mouth within an exclusive circle. Many jobs were not even published, so unless you were part of that inner circle, you wouldn't even know there was an opening.

But networking doesn't have to be an exclusive bunch of insiders sharing information to the exclusion of others. It's also about building genuine relationships, connecting with people who share similar interests or goals, and mutually supporting each other.

Networking can be a positive and empowering experience that opens doors and creates opportunities not just for you but for your friends and peers as well. If we examine networking through a friendlier lens, it becomes more of a beneficial practice and less of an onerous chore.

So, even if you're just starting out, now is a great time to embrace networking and start building your own network of supportive connections.

Don't let negative connotations associated with networking hold you back.

Today, the landscape of networking is rapidly evolving. Thanks to technology, it's no longer just about who you know because now everyone can potentially connect with anyone. Social media platforms like LinkedIn have made it easier than ever to establish and maintain professional relationships.

Ivan Misner, a networking expert, emphasizes building genuine, long-term relationships based on trust and reciprocity. It's not about collecting business cards or making superficial connections. It's less about going for the kill and landing a job referral or recommendation and more about nurturing relationships for the long term.

"Networking is not about hunting, it's about farming," Misner says.[1]

And like farming, networking requires consistency and persistence. It's not a one-time thing but a process of making efforts to meet people, following up with e-mails or calls, and staying engaged with your network over time.

Networking requires that you do some weeding and watering to grow a supportive crop of people willing to help you when help is needed.

The transactional nature of networking—asking for favors, referrals, or jobs—is what leaves a bad taste in our mouths.

But there's a difference between networking and opportunism. Networking is developing a cohort of people willing to support you. Opportunism is trying to get something that you don't deserve.

You can do a lot to begin to develop your network. And much of it is easy!

For example, you should stay in touch with your high school teachers. Many of them have spent an entire year in a classroom with you, monitoring and tracking your abilities, strengths, and aspirations. Few people in your life know you as well as they do.

Yet many students, once the end of the school year hits, never really stay in touch with the people who know the most about them or care the most about how well they do—teachers have invested a lot of time in helping shape you both academically and socially. It would make sense that seeing the fruits of their labor would be a huge treat.

So start now. Keep your teachers—especially those who teach subjects that are of interest to you—firmly in your life. You don't have to be at the top of the class or even very involved in the class. Teachers want to help; that's why they became teachers. Seek them out, difficult as that might be if you're shy or a poor student. Tell them where you're thinking of going to college, and even after you've graduated, visit them when you return home for vacations.

Teachers are among the most generous people on the planet. Drop by their class and say hello! They gravitate toward the profession precisely *because* they care about young people and want to know what happens in their lives.

And you know who else cares about you? Your school counselor. Stay in touch and let them know what's going on in your life. Counselors can continue to provide support, too, if you decide to transfer to another university.

They'll likely be able to teach you a thing or two about how to network as well. School counselors are master networkers because the better their relationships with university admissions folks, the more effectively they can advocate for qualified student applicants. So, whether you are in high school or have graduated, your counselors are a valuable resource for both your mind and your heart.

You'll be amazed at how good it will feel to have such supportive people in your network. In addition, you might be surprised at all the talents and abilities of your teachers and counselors. Just because those sides of them weren't apparent during high school doesn't mean they didn't have interests that made them even more fascinating people!

And on that topic, sometimes people network to feel good about themselves. It can be as simple as that!

Think about the last time you helped an elderly person cross the street or carry groceries to their car. Or maybe you volunteered at a food pantry serving Thanksgiving dinner to struggling families or even just talked a friend through a personal problem that was getting them down.

You probably felt pretty good afterward not only about solving a problem but also about yourself as a person. That's because humans are inherently social beings, and helping someone in need can activate your brain's reward system and release "feel-good" chemicals like dopamine. It's the same thing that happens when you eat something delicious.

Helping people also gives you a sense of purpose and meaning, which enhances your sense of self-worth and fulfillment.

So people want to help others just because it feels good!

There are more reasons why networking can be a positive thing.

The "Ben Franklin effect," a psychological phenomenon named after the statesman and founding father, suggests that building relationships is a reciprocal process. When we do a favor or help someone, we tend to develop a positive perception of that person and are more likely to continue engaging with them in a positive manner.

As a result, we go out of our way to provide value, such as sharing resources or providing support. This creates a sense of goodwill and reciprocity, meaning that people *want* to help you. You just have to let them.

While there may still be some perception of certain schools or professions having stronger alumni networks, the reality is that the landscape of networking has changed. It is no longer solely about the schools you go to. The playing field has been leveled by technology, making networking more accessible and inclusive for everyone.

When going to college wasn't as common as it is now, the focus was on whether you went to a prestigious university. But today, as higher education has become more widespread and accessible, companies care less about the name of your school than they did in the past.

Going to a top-ranked school and slacking off may not guarantee success, while attending a community college and excelling could lead to great opportunities. Of course, many jobs still require a college degree, but outside of a few fields, the importance of where you went to school has certainly diminished.

At big schools, there may not be as strong a sense of community. At Texas A&M University, one of the country's biggest public universities, there are 58,269 undergraduate enrollments. With that vast student population, it may be harder to feel a sense of connection with your classmates.

On the other hand, Swarthmore College in Pennsylvania and California's Claremont McKenna College each have fewer than 2,000 students. These schools may foster a stronger bond among alumni simply because of the intimacy of smaller numbers of graduates.

With the rise of remote work and busy schedules, networking has shifted from in-person interactions to quicker, online connections. Relationships can begin and flourish virtually. Of course, in person is always best not only because you can more personally engage with a contact but also because you can read their body language and better understand their level of interest. You are able to "read" a person better when you see them face-to-face.

Either way, many people are not proactive in asking for help or providing tangible ways for others to help them.

There may also be a tendency to rely solely on online job boards to avoid the perceived awkwardness of networking. Simply sending messages that you've copied from ChatGPT to strangers on LinkedIn isn't necessarily effective networking. You need to do research about the work that people do and how that might provide some connective tissue with your own aspirations.

Prior to applying to college, seek out professors and establish relationships with the ones you admire. Look beyond faculty to people in the field you are interested in. If you're studying film, reach out to local filmmakers. If you're studying accounting, find the most successful accountant in town and ask them out for coffee simply to pick their brain.

You have no idea where that kind of networking can lead, and often it's toward something positive.

Networking is a powerful tool that can propel you to new heights!

And a good networker doesn't necessarily need to have been the best student academically or the highest achiever. People who are good at networking are skilled at building and nurturing relationships in high school, maybe getting along with students in various cliques and with different interests. And in the business world, those kinds of abilities are valued, as they can translate into how well someone can manage clients or drive sales.

Charlie Chang, an entrepreneur, is a YouTuber who asks accomplished people about the secrets to their success. Often the ability to fearlessly schmooze is mentioned as a strength.

"Without being able to socialize and network and talk to people, you won't be able to take it to the next level," said one entrepreneur who was interviewed while attending the Coachella music festival. "I'd take that ability to network and socialize over anything else."

The initial discomfort people have with networking can't be an obstacle. "You have to put yourself out there," the entrepreneur added. "Everyone has certain fears that you need to overcome, and you just have got to go and do it."

And as networking gains importance, a wider variety of candidates can access job opportunities due to efforts rooted in technology.

Take Handshake, a jobs portal designed for recent university graduates. With 18 million students and graduates on Handshake and Fortune 500 companies signed up to look for new hires there, the potential for connecting with influential professionals is immense.

"My co-founders and I started Handshake to ensure that *all* students are able to find meaningful jobs, regardless of where they're from or where they go to school," wrote Garrett Lord, CEO and cofounder, on the company's blog.[2] He added that the company's mission is "democratizing opportunity for all students."

The company's valuation of $3.5 billion is a testament to its success despite the three founders being alumni of Michigan Technological University (currently ranked 779th in the *U.S. News & World Report*'s "Best Global Universities"[3] and 151st in the magazine's "Best National Universities" ranking).[4]

And don't underestimate what you can bring to the table.

In fact, you can even be a mentor!

Diya Khanna, a global diversity, equity, and inclusion consultant, says that "reverse mentorship"[5] is a term to describe when older, more experienced individuals learn from younger, less experienced workers. This shift in dynamics reflects the rapidly changing world of technology and culture of the modern workplace.

However, it's important to note that simply being part of an alumni network, whether it be Dartmouth College, Denison University, or De Anza College, is not enough to produce any kind of substantive result.

Networking requires intentional effort and strategy. Taking a page from the MBA handbook, even if you've just started college, can be a wise move. Adam Grant, the youngest tenured professor at the University of Pennsylvania's Wharton School of Business[6] and author of the *New York Times* bestseller *Give and Take,* emphasizes the benefits of providing more value to others than you expect in return.

As a "giver," Grant says, you should focus on contributing to others without seeking anything in return.

So, if you selflessly help your classmates and peers, they in turn will see you as a valuable resource. This reputation will create opportunities after graduation as your peers look to reciprocate your generosity by helping you potentially land an internship or meet a prospective mentor.

Deliberately planting seeds early is key rather than simply fantasizing about your future when you graduate. As the job market becomes increasingly challenging and strategic, the process of connecting with alumni should start earlier than you think.

Networking is more about gathering information and building relationships than about simply trying to get a recommendation or a job. Approaching it as a process rather than a means to an end can help you develop the necessary comfort level when reaching out to strangers.

By tapping into their preexisting relationships, like with teachers, students can explore their areas of interest, discover available opportunities, and gain valuable advice. Establishing connections with individuals already known to them serves as an excellent stepping stone for those embarking on their journey to secure a full-time position.

In the world of networking, it's often the entry-level workers who feel uncomfortable and hesitant to engage, while powerful people know they can grant favors and opportunities that are of value to many.

However, no matter how you feel about it, networking is crucial for career growth, and low-power players can take steps to overcome their discomfort.

Before engaging in a networking event, one strategy is to shift focus from what you can gain to what you can contribute. It doesn't have to be something big. Think about your own abilities and existing network, and you'll likely find something of value to offer.

For example, you could propose conducting a personal campus tour for the child of a senior executive who is interested in your university. Or maybe you could organize a focus group of your Generation Z friends for a marketing executive you'd like to meet.

Creativity, resourcefulness, and initiative can go a long way in networking.

Even if your offer is declined, at least you'll have shown your willingness to contribute, and you might make a key connection and feel valued in the process.

As former presidential candidate and New York mayoral contender Andrew Yang once tweeted, "When someone is good to you, you instinctively want to return the favor."

Giving can lead to receiving in the world of networking.

While being qualified and well informed remains a prerequisite for tapping into networks for internships and jobs, employers are casting a wider net for new recruits as they strive for increased diversity in their workforces, enhancing access to networking opportunities for those from underrepresented groups.

In particular, LinkedIn has remained true to its roots as a platform for professional development. You don't have to be directly connected to ask a question of a senior executive or request a conversation, which makes it easier to initiate interactions with professionals of interest.

In today's dynamic job market, changing positions and locations multiple times, even changing fields, is common. Being comfortable with this fluidity and letting people know about your career changes can open up new networking opportunities.

In fact, staying in one place for too long may raise more questions than changing jobs frequently does.

Sure, some of networking's unappealing relics remain in place. Those in power tend to protect their power and so have every reason to preserve exclusive circles.

But other than that, networking has become more accessible and diverse. The traditional idea of networking taking place in a hotel ballroom with the goal of collecting as many business cards as possible is quickly fading and holds little appeal to young people who feel like they have nothing to offer.

Instead, focus on meeting people for the sake of genuine connections and relationships, and they may help your career in surprising ways. Even casual conversations and random encounters can lead to unexpected but welcome outcomes.

Getting an internship might be a focus of yours right now. You can approach that in the same manner people do jobs—it can mean connecting with people in your school or community who might be able to put you in touch with their own networks. Be proactive in reaching out and offer to share your own skills, knowledge, or perspectives with them.

And, increasingly, a successful internship experience can lead to a job offer. For example, college marketing representatives for record companies are college students—or recent graduates—who work part-time to publicize label artists among a young adult demographic. In doing so, they gain firsthand marketing experience. By being such a representative—also known as campus representatives or college and lifestyle marketing representatives—a student can also figure out if this is an attractive career.

By having these programs, music companies, such as Sony Music or Universal Music Group, build recruitment pipelines that lead to full-time jobs. So both employer and intern can benefit! Networking to speak to former reps about their experiences can be a good way to get your foot in the door.

Also, phone or video calls can be valuable for making more personal and direct connections. While you can use technology and social media platforms to keep abreast of business trends and the promotions of connections, sometimes it makes a difference to hear a human voice!

And even if the internships or work experience that you gain aren't necessarily the ones you had initially wanted, nothing is ever a mistake. By doing a wide variety of things, you have the opportunity to learn about what you don't like, which is as important as discovering what you enjoy.

You gain skills and knowledge with all that you do and broaden your network of friends and colleagues. So just focus on learning and building your skills and your network. With the right mindset, you can create a fulfilling path forward.

And, as Ben Franklin might advise, don't be afraid to let others help you along the way!

10

MAYBE YOU DON'T NEED TO GO TO COLLEGE AT ALL

As a high school student, you have undoubtedly heard adults talking about the importance of getting a college degree. They may have told you that a college education is the key to a successful career and a better life.

And generally, that holds true. The point of this book is to highlight how that's the case, especially if you take control over what you decide to do.

But there's a trend toward not needing a university degree to get a job.[1] And that trend is gaining traction as fast-moving technology continues to influence the direction of economic growth. Not needing a degree is not the same as not needing an education—but you can now get that education in many ways.

Technology is developing at a breathtakingly rapid pace, at a speed never before seen. That might sound a bit overblown, but it's not. These days, writing about technology is like trying to capture lightning in a bottle. Maybe you've heard that idiom, but it means trying to catch or hold on to something that is extremely elusive and quickly changing.

When describing technology, referring to lightning, too, is appropriate. Lightning is a powerful and unpredictable phenomenon, which also reflects the potency of technology.

Right now, you're using ChatGPT and other AI-powered tools to help you write, summarize, and do other tasks. The potential for technology to revolutionize the way people learn is almost unfathomably vast, and you and your friends will be helping the universities you attend in trying to figure out what that transformation is going to look like.

But the changes in the workforce will be equally profound. In fact, the completeness with which entire industries will be overhauled has left people wondering how things are going to look next year, much less in five or 10 years.

Before AI became mainstream, many task-based jobs were already being automated. We're talking jobs that involve repetitive tasks, such as working on a factory line, telemarketing, and collecting tolls.

Much of that was due to the development of robotics. In the case of factory lines, for example, robotics was especially attractive.

Think about an automobile factory, where cars move along a conveyor, passing through different stations for assembly, inspection, and testing before being prepared for shipment. Even if the process is meticulously organized, the potential for injuries remains. With factory workers using tools that can cut or puncture, lifting heavy components, and using chemicals like solvents and paints, the potential for hurting oneself is pretty evident. Even with training and protective equipment, risks exist.

But if those factory line tasks are automated, the precision of tasks becomes more standardized with fewer injuries to worry about. Fewer mishaps mean less liability for factory managers as well as increased productivity because robots don't need vacation days.

It also means fewer jobs on factory lines for human beings.

Similarly, the number of jobs at brick-and-mortar stores has declined as online shopping has become more popular. Technology that enabled e-commerce on websites such as Amazon is behind all those empty storefronts you see in your local mall or downtown commercial district.

Since then, a significant advancement known as "supervised learning" has emerged. It involves training an AI system to recognize patterns or make decisions by providing it with numerous pre-labeled examples that serve as correct answers, enabling the AI to learn from them and independently tackle similar problems.

This has helped replace human workers tasked with more service-oriented tasks. Examples are numerous, including data entry clerks responsible for extracting and entering data from documents, customer service representatives answering common customer questions and scheduling appointments, and medical staff responsible for analyzing X-rays and MRI scans for abnormalities.

However, now, with generative AI, the workforce will not only be further streamlined but also completely rethought: complicated law cases figured out in a matter of seconds, negotiations with vendors that used to take weeks now taking a matter of days, television screenplays written in the style of well-known writers or based on previous popular shows, term papers and tests graded quickly and accurately with lessons taught to each student's ability and learning style.

AI can replicate the catchy refrains of songs or mimic the way people sing. It can reproduce the painting techniques of famous artists and write in the style of an esteemed novelist.

And we're just at the beginning of this potential revolution in work.

So the question is, what role does a university degree play in an environment where the parameters are not yet drawn?

Certainly, AI will help create efficiency. You've probably experienced that firsthand, with ChatGPT helping you with your assignments, whether it be to answer questions, draft essays, create summaries of readings, or teach you simple computer code.

But as was the case in the past, it is unclear if a college degree will get you in the door of greater opportunity in this context.

So let's start with the obvious.

If you're interested in making a living as a professional YouTuber or TikToker, there is absolutely no need to have a university degree. What you need are ideas, energy, access to a mobile phone, and dedication to regularly churn out content.

In this profession, to spend four years in classrooms not only seems like a waste of time but may actually work against getting traction in these careers.

Some people say we're living in an "attention economy," a term[2] that was originally defined by psychologist and economist Herbert A. Simon. Attention is seen as a kind of currency in our social media–obsessed, information-saturated world and is what influencers seek to earn in the same way most people earn salaries. Successful YouTubers use their skills to create engrossing videos and vlogs and need the discipline to continue doing so for years at a time.

The majority of you will likely not be seeking careers making videos, but so much of what we do these days—from going to a party with friends to getting into college—is commemorated by a social media post that is approved of via "likes." That is a sign of participation in an "attention economy."

The bar of entry for participation is low, at least initially, and it certainly doesn't require a university degree.

At the same time, we are becoming an increasingly skills-based economy, and skills-based hiring is on the rise. If you're being hired for a particular skill that you have, that doesn't necessarily require a four-year degree, either.

For example, many manufacturing jobs require technical skills and certifications that can be obtained through vocational programs or on-the-job training.

Similarly, many health care jobs, such as medical assistant, dental hygienist, and respiratory therapist, require only an associate degree or certificate.

Another reason why young people can get good jobs without a university degree is the rise of entrepreneurship and the gig economy. With the advent of technology, it has become easier for people to start their businesses or work as freelancers, independent contractors, or consultants.

For example, many young people are finding success as app developers, graphic designers, content creators, or social media managers, often without having a college degree. And this is happening as the cost of a college education has become prohibitively expensive for many young people—according to the U.S. Bureau of Labor Statistics, the average cost of tuition and fees at public four-year institutions has risen by 32 percent over the past decade.[3]

In addition, there are many states and employers that have lifted requirements for job applicants to have a university degree. One such example is the state of Colorado, which in 2020 passed a law that removes the degree requirement for certain state government jobs. Under this new law, job applicants will be evaluated based on their skills, experience, and competency rather than their educational credentials.

The state of Pennsylvania also removed requirements for a four-year college degree from most state government jobs, as have Maryland and Utah.

Similarly, major employers like Google, Apple, and IBM have also removed the degree requirement[4] for many of their positions. Google announced in 2018 that it would no longer require a college degree for its entry-level software engineering jobs, citing the need to expand its talent pool and promote diversity and inclusion in its hiring practices.[5]

Who knows better what Google is looking for in potential hires than Google itself?

If working at Google is your dream, you might better your odds by earning a "Google Career Certificate." The company leapfrogged universities by providing the training for the skills they need to build their own workforce.

The online training covers user experience, design project management, and data analytics and skills for other tech-related jobs. The certificates don't cost much, require no previous experience, and are bundled with interview tips and professional connections to more than 150 companies working with Google. And you don't need a college degree.

The company has chosen fields that can be taught effectively online and teaches skills that are in demand and for which one is paid well.

Google says there are 2.4 million job postings across certificate fields with a median salary across the fields of $76,000.[6]

Suggesting that companies like Google are the future of education is obviously overly simplistic. But what Google has done indicates two things: (1) the company isn't finding university graduates with the skills they are looking for, and (2) they aren't waiting around for higher education to pay attention and change.

In the past, many employers have traditionally asked for a degree when one was not needed simply because the state of the labor market often permitted it. Transparency about the skills and level of education required for the job means maximizing opportunities for all and managing expectations of those who are applying.

Why shouldn't those companies provide their own tailored training that produces professionals who can, from the get-go, perform the exact tasks they need to be competitive?

Other companies, like EY, Hilton Worldwide, and Whole Foods, have also eliminated degree requirements for certain roles, recognizing that a college education is not always a predictor of success in the workplace. Different jobs require different types of skills, levels, and types of education.

There can also be a variety of employment opportunities under a single corporate brand. An example is professional services company Accenture. Many associate Accenture as a desirable destination for college- or even MBA-educated hotshots who are hired to advise clients on how to run their businesses better.

But Accenture also has apprenticeship programs to provide on-the-job training and career development opportunities for young people that "are redefining the future of talent and creating a more inclusive innovation economy."[7]

This is part of an overall trend of apprenticeship growth in the United States.[8] Apprenticeships typically involve a combination of hands-on work, classroom instruction, and mentorship, allowing individuals to develop practical expertise while earning a wage or stipend.

Overall, the movement toward removing degree requirements for jobs is gaining momentum as employers recognize the value of skills, experience, and diversity in the workplace. By opening up opportunities to a broader pool of candidates, employers can tap into a wider range of talents and perspectives and build a more dynamic and innovative workforce.

At the same time, corporate leaders are openly questioning the need for higher education at all. Some say that millions of jobs requiring a four-year college degree can be done without attaining that level of academic study.

In fact, some executives advise that companies shake up their approach to hiring and employ unconventional candidates without degrees who have potential and train them.

"It's really important for us to recognize that because people haven't had an opportunity early in their lives, it doesn't mean that they can't make a real contribution to your company," said Kenneth Frazier, the former CEO of Merck & Co.[9]

While Frazier and other corporate leaders support traditional college education for some people, they say that many entry-level positions don't need it. Cloud programmers, cybersecurity analysts, financial operations specialists, and many health care jobs can all begin without a college degree, with applicants given the option to get more education later.

"By making a four-year degree a prerequisite for hiring, we are creating structural barriers to economic opportunity," said Ginni Rometty, former CEO of IBM, a company that has dropped many degree requirements for job applicants in recent years.[10]

Rometty noted that over time and with training, "new-collar" employees, as she called those without a four-year degree, had performance results that were equal to or better than those of workers with a traditional education.

And that's IBM—about as established and traditional as they come.

Even the federal government no longer requires a university degree of its job applicants. So, if your dream is to shake up the government, *go for it!*

In May 2021, Reuters news agency launched a free e-learning program in partnership with Facebook to support journalists in certain parts of the world with digital reporting and editing training. The program provides "the foundation for sound journalism, whether you're a budding journalist or a seasoned one looking for a refresher."[11]

Certainly, learning from Reuters and Facebook may be more appealing than committing to a master's program in journalism at an elite university, at least from the perspective of cost. Columbia University, for example, estimates that the "all-in" cost of its nine-and-a-half-month master's program in journalism would be $126,683—with tuition costing $75,348, fees $9,513, and living expenses $41,822.[12]

Now compare that cost with what a fledgling journalist might make in terms of salary.

According to the U.S. Bureau of Labor Statistics, the annual mean wage of news analysts, reporters, and journalists in the overall newspaper and print business is $54,270, while those in radio and television broadcasting have an annual mean wage of $75,140.[13]

In an economy that is becoming more skills based and automated, universities will come under increased pressure to make their graduates more employable—and if they fail to do so, fast-moving companies like Google will circumvent them and take on that role themselves.

At the same time, there's a shortage of workers with what might be described as tradespeople or craftsmen—people who work in a skilled trade, such as carpentry, plumbing, electrical work, welding, or automotive repair.

These alarm bells over these scarcities have been sounding for years now!

There are active shortages of around 500,000 construction workers,[14] 600,000 auto technicians,[15] and 800,000 manufacturing roles.[16] In addition, there's a scarcity of carpenters—400,000 unfilled jobs.[17]

Because of these scarcities, we are seeing a shift in tradespeople tides.

Recent enrollment data from the National Student Clearinghouse Research Center shows that trade school interest is on the up-and-up, with double-digit increases in many vocational programs, including mechanic, repair, construction, and culinary courses.

This contrasts with two- and four-year college enrollment, which is on a downward trend (7.8 and 3.4 percent, respectively, for public programs).[18]

These numbers partially represent a pandemic rebound—as hands-on fields strained to offer hands-on training during the COVID crisis, enrollments in the trades dropped. But that's not the entire story here.

Young people are choosing trade schools over degree programs because it's just more financially practical at this point, according to *The Hechinger Report*.[19]

The Washington State auditor found that an education at a public university was twice as expensive as a technical education, while private universities were 10 times more costly.[20]

But regardless of the financial reasons why trade schools might be gaining popularity, the main one is this—the promise of getting a job!

Federal data show that trade school students are more likely to be employed after school than their high-spending university counterparts—and much more likely to work in their fields of study as well.

Those trade jobs are paying well, too. According to Georgetown University's *Good Jobs Project*,[21] many of these are among the 30 million jobs paying $55,000 per year that don't require a four-year degree.

So there are a few important conclusions to be drawn here.

The first is that, in today's tech-driven economy, the traditional path of obtaining a university degree in order to secure a high-paying job is no longer the only option. In fact, a good number of successful people in the tech industry today are self-taught or have obtained their education through nontraditional channels.

The tech industry is constantly evolving, and new technologies are emerging all the time. This means that employers are often looking for candidates who are adaptable, curious, and willing to learn on the job. They are also often willing to invest in employees who have a strong technical skill set and have the ability to work collaboratively in a team environment.

These qualities are not necessarily tied to a university degree.

But a university degree can't be beat in terms of providing a valuable foundation of knowledge and encouraging curiosity. In addition, the salary premium placed on a university degree remains firmly in place, even as companies increasingly hire workers with specific skills or decide to provide training to develop those skills in existing employees.

So it's up to you to decide whether to pursue a university degree or take a more nontraditional path. The most important thing is that you develop the technical skills, adaptability, and curiosity that are essential to succeed in today's dizzyingly evolving world!

11

THE HARD TRUTH BEHIND HIGHER EDUCATION

We're living in a world of contradictions right now.

Ivy League universities and their ilk are being flooded with record-high numbers of applications. As a result, their acceptance rates continue to narrow to a nearly unthinkable degree.

By the looks of the tidal wave of interest in these institutions, you'd conclude that going to college must be the goal of high school students everywhere.

That's not exactly the case.

Overall, higher education enrollments have been on a declining trend. According to one survey, 74 percent of colleges are facing financial challenges, with smaller schools more likely to be facing trouble.[1] Among the surveyed schools with fewer than 5,000 students, 79 percent said financial constraints were a problem.

Bigger schools didn't fare that much better, with 52 percent of colleges or universities with more than 30,000 students saying they were feeling the pinch.

Contrary to what's going on with their more famous counterparts, many universities and colleges just can't get students to enroll.

In the fall of 2021, total undergraduate enrollment in degree-granting postsecondary institutions in the United States fell 3 percent when compared to the fall of 2020. Overall, undergraduate enrollments were 15 percent lower in the fall of 2021 than in the fall of 2010, with 42 percent of this decline occurring during the pandemic.[2]

Things are particularly bad at community colleges, which have seen enrollments drop significantly as well.[3]

While university enrollments have stabilized recently, they are still much lower than pre-pandemic levels. We're talking 1.23 million undergraduates fewer compared to the fall of 2019. Freshman enrollments alone are down by 150,000 compared to 2019. That's a lot.

The reasons for these declines are numerous.

One is kind of basic. There are fewer students enrolling at universities because there are just fewer students. There has been a historic decline in the number of total public school enrollments between the fall of 2019 and the fall of 2020.[4]

This leads to fewer high school–aged students and then even fewer who decide to go to college.

There is not much anyone can do about a student population decline.

Another factor is that high school graduates have been opting to go to work rather than to college. Before the pandemic, the economy was pretty robust, so wages were pretty good.

People wanted to start making money after graduation rather than taking on debt to go to college. Without a clear idea about what to study, students took the route that made the most sense to them.

The pandemic didn't help matters. In some households, parents lost their jobs, so that put even more pressure on students to make money to help make ends meet. Some chose college as the best way forward, but others selected other pathways.

Today, there are different reasons why high school graduates are choosing work over higher education. One of them, as discussed earlier, is to go directly into a trade.

In some people's eyes, becoming plumbers, electricians, or nursing assistants was not as lofty a goal as heading to college.

But when your sink backs up and pouring Drano in the drain doesn't work, when your dad turns on the electric water kettle at the same time as the microwave and blows a fuse, or when your grandmother falls in her house and has to go to the ER, you realize how valuable these professionals are.

One of the biggest reasons why students don't pursue a university education is because of cost. And that can often lead to debt.

In some countries, such as Germany, Sweden, Denmark, and Finland, a university education is free (or close to it). Countries like the United Kingdom also once offered a basically free university education. Even though many of the universities in those countries charge tuition fees, they are still generally less expensive than the fees in the United States for domestic students.

The idea behind a free university education is that access to higher education should be fair and equitable. And the better educated a country's population is, the better off that country can be.

That, of course, is a noble concept. And in countries where the government can financially support the higher-education system, tuition can be kept at a minimum.

But in the United States, this isn't the case, and tuition is a major—and necessary—revenue source for universities.

For those of you interested in studying at a university in the United States, here's one piece of advice: avoid deep debt.

For many students, going to college isn't possible without taking on some loans. So let's just say, when it comes to debt, don't get buried in it.

Do some research and pursue majors that will result in an outcome that will be satisfactory for you: if you're going into debt, make sure that the education you're buying will allow you to pay back that debt in a reasonable amount of time.

Unlike generations of students in the past, data are available that can help you figure that out! As discussed in earlier chapters, you can go into college knowing how much you'll likely make in terms of a starting salary when you graduate.

That's not to say that money you'll potentially earn should be the determining factor for all you do at school. There are a lot of benefits to going to college that go beyond the tangible—the independence you'll gain living away from home, the time management skills you'll acquire being responsible for running your own life, and the network of peers you develop—so don't view the experience through a narrow lens.

But by the same token, do what you can to inform yourself in terms of debt versus salary outcomes.

Don't just close your eyes and take the leap.

Today, more than half of students leave campus burdened with debt. The total is $1.75 trillion (including federal and private loans), which means $28,950 owed per borrower on average.[5]

States with the Highest and Lowest Average Student Debt

Highest-debt states		Lowest-debt states	
New Hampshire	$39,928	Utah	$18,344
Delaware	$39,705	New Mexico	$20,868
Pennsylvania	$39,375	California	$21,125
Rhode Island	$36,791	Nevada	$21,357
Connecticut	$35,853	Wyoming	$23,510

Source: "Student Debt and the Class of 2020," *The Institute for College Access & Success*, https://ticas.org/wp-content/uploads/2021/11/classof2020.pdf (June 21, 2023).

Fifty-five percent of students from public four-year institutions had student loans, and 57 percent of students from private nonprofit four-year institutions took on education debt.

That's a lot of debt!

This debt can be particularly challenging for students who do not complete their degrees or who face limited job prospects after graduation. Many borrowers struggle to make their loan payments, with high levels of delinquency and default.

Look at how states compare when it comes to debt.

There are many contributing factors as to why some states tend to be higher when it comes to student debt. One might be that some states simply have more universities and students than other states. This could mean, too, that there's less state aid that needs to be spread across more students.

Changes in federal policy have made it easier for students to borrow money but have also reduced the availability of grant-based aid that does not need to be repaid. Moreover, the pandemic has exacerbated student debt, as many borrowers have faced financial challenges due to job losses or reduced income.

Meanwhile, college tuition and fees have been skyrocketing over the past few decades, making it harder and harder for students to afford college—or, at least, that's what the headlines are telling you.

Sometimes those frightening headlines about how much tuition has been rising are a bit misleading. The tuition fees being referred to are known as the "sticker price" or the "list price," which means those are the publicly facing tuition fees that are on a university's website.

In reality, a small percentage of students pay that full price.

According to a study by the National Association of College and University Business Officers, the vast majority—82.5 percent—of undergraduates received grant aid in the 2021–2022 academic year.[6] Many students at private colleges do not pay the full published tuition and fees. In fact, the average amount of financial aid awarded was the highest it's ever been, covering 60.7 percent of the published tuition and fees.

What's sad, though, is that many students don't know about this discounting and so don't even bother to apply to schools they think will be too expensive for their budgets.

Why are colleges discounting their tuition?

Because they need to fill their freshman seats. It helps students who otherwise could not afford to attend college. Enrollment declines have had a significant impact on the financial health of many universities and colleges. With fewer students, institutions are facing reduced revenue and increased financial pressure, leading to budget cuts, layoffs, and program closures.

According to a report by Moody's Investors Service, declines in the number of high school graduates and competition from online programs will increase the financial risk of U.S. colleges.[7]

Universities know, too, that there are many families who can't afford their publicized tuition fees. And, at the same time, universities are facing a growing number of people who question the value of a college degree.

According to a recent study, nearly a third of parents and students believe that the cost of a college education outweighs its value.[8] In addition, 81 percent of families had eliminated a school from their list based on the high cost.

So why don't universities just lower their tuition fees?

There's a thing called the "Chivas Regal" effect. The reference to the blended Scotch whiskey is the belief that the more expensive something is, the better its quality. In other words, price equals quality.

So, due to the Chivas Regal effect, some colleges raise their tuition prices every year or so.[9] But to enroll prospects, they use financial hardship or merit to discount fees for students they want but who cannot afford full fare.

They also provide scholarships to high achievers—both athletic and academic—whom they want to recruit.

There are universities where literally no one pays the publicized tuition fee. At Colby-Sawyer College in New Hampshire, for example, every student got a discount. That discounting practice eventually led to the college just cutting its official tuition fee for the 2023–2024 academic year from about $46,000 to $17,500, an official discount of 62 percent.[10]

Colby-Sawyer said their ability to discount and cut fees was due to years of strategic planning and efforts to strengthen the institution's financial stability.

So you have an idea about the swashbuckling nature of college finances today!

But the problems aren't limited to the cost of college. We're talking about the relevance of a college degree.

Many colleges and universities are struggling to provide students with the education they need to succeed in today's job market. They may offer outdated curricula that don't reflect the needs of modern industries. They may not have enough resources to provide students with hands-on experience or access to cutting-edge technology.

And they may not be preparing students for the real-world challenges they'll face after graduation.

That lack of relevance leads to what is referred to as a "skills gap." The skills that university students graduate with don't align with the skills employers need to build their workforces, thus creating a gap.

According to some experts, companies are having an increasingly hard time attracting and keeping employees who have the skills they need to fill open positions. Among 600 U.S. human resource professionals surveyed by a research firm, 69 percent said their organization had a skills gap, higher than the 55 percent in a similar 2021 survey.[11]

This means that what universities are teaching students doesn't necessarily correlate with what's going on in industry.

In addition, this gap might translate into student dissatisfaction with what they studied. In fact, nearly two in five American college graduates have major regrets, and those regrets generally fall along the line of liberal arts versus STEM.

As a rule, those who studied STEM subjects are much more likely to believe they made the right choice. Conversely, those in social sciences or vocational courses second-guess themselves.

According to a Federal Reserve survey, nearly half of humanities and arts majors had remorse about their major as of 2021.[12] Engineering majors had the fewest regrets, with just 24 percent wishing they had chosen something different.

Looking at the Fed data, you can conclude that the higher your income is today, the less you regret the major you chose back in college.

The Federal Reserve's annual Survey of Household Economics and Decisionmaking also asks if people regret the school they went to.[13]

Those in vocational programs are most likely to regret their school, while education majors are least likely.

The regret for those in vocational programs might relate to how people with university degrees tend to make more money over their lifetimes than those who don't. A substantial majority of vocational and technical students, 60 percent, wish they'd gone for more schooling, while less than 40 percent of law, life science, and engineering students believe the same.

Regardless of major, half of those who went to private, for-profit schools regret their decision, perhaps because students at for-profit schools are much more likely to struggle to repay their student debt.

Similar regrets plague only 21 percent of those who went to public colleges and universities and 30 percent of those who attended private nonprofits. This might mean that most graduates from these schools thought their investment was worth it.

While it is true that some STEM majors earn more than some humanities majors, a number of the highest-earning humanities majors earn more than the lowest-earning STEM majors.

This may be because humanities majors teach critical thinking, which allows students to adapt to jobs that may not have existed when they enrolled in college. And, as you are aware, the skills needed to manage AI and to be an adept "prompt engineer" can rest to a great degree on your critical thinking ability.

So, beyond your college applications, the business of higher education is complicated. But by understanding the context within which you are operating, you can make a better-informed decision about the pathway you decide to take.

In the navy, there is a common phrase that goes "you have the conn." This phrase comes from a long-standing navy tradition that grants only one officer in charge the authority to give orders to the helmsman about the ship's speed and direction.

The primary goal is to ensure clarity and avoid any confusion about who is in command of the ship at any given time.

So, despite the complexity of the world around you, never forget who is in charge.

You have the conn!

A FUTURE WHERE ANYTHING IS POSSIBLE

Before we look ahead toward your future, let's take inventory of what's going on right now when it comes to a university education.

Some scenarios will stay the same. Think of them as the stones in a stream—no matter how free a current is, the water must flow around them.

One of those immovable stones is anxiety. You might even characterize this persistent feeling as fear, a foreboding sense that one isn't doing enough to get into the right place or to even get in anywhere.

We're talking about concerns about admission and about paying for the cost of a university education.

And that's not simply about the hundreds of thousands of applications being sent to the country's top universities. As preoccupying as that may be, how you are feeling about college admissions is more than just the application tidal wave.

In the spring of 2023, a high school senior in New Orleans with a 4.98 GPA was accepted to around 130 colleges and universities and received $9 million in scholarship offers.[1]

Now if that's not a record, it's got to be close to one!

Perhaps even more striking is his completing around 200 applications to schools across the country. How a student could accomplish that—on top of homework and school activities—is truly mind-bending.

In addition, before graduating high school, this student earned 27 college credits.

Without a doubt, from an ambition and determination standpoint, this achievement is to be applauded (and the student eventually decided to go to Cornell University, so congratulations!). That goes without saying. But for teenagers to even think of putting themselves through such duress to ensure opportunity—while dealing with the usual high school stresses, both academic and social, no less—doesn't seem right.

In fact, it seems downright unfair.

Undoubtedly, trying to improve your odds is a good strategy. Perhaps you're doing that by applying to a varied mix of both public and private universities. It's wise to cover enough of your "safety" schools so you're ensured of a place while at the same time shooting high for those "reach" universities to maximize your chances of getting in.

By preparing for every possibility and paying attention to every facet of a situation, you better your chances for success.

But there's also the saying about having "too many irons in the fire."

That saying, which dates to the mid-1500s, is derived from black-smithing. If a blacksmith attempts to heat too many pieces of iron in the fire at once, it cools the fire, and none of the pieces of iron will heat sufficiently.

By doing too many things, you can sap yourself of energy and prevent yourself from seeing the overall picture and, as a result, which path to take. So, while applying to a huge number of schools technically increases the likelihood of acceptances, a better approach might be to research your options and base your applications on your goals.

And your goals should extend beyond the universities that accept you. Think about what you want to do and the person you want to become.

Universities will continue their marketing efforts. They need to keep their enrollments up as well as have a large enough applicant pool from which they can choose the best possible students. And continued competition will lead to more students applying, at least to select universities.

But don't worry! As discussed in this book, the way people look at a university education is shifting. Change is definitely afoot.

Chess.com, the online chess platform that allows players from across the globe to play chess, learn from videos, and participate in tournaments, posted an open application for a CEO position. Aside from criteria such as having more than 10 years of management experience in tech or gaming, the website specified that the leader of the world's largest chess community must "not have an MBA from Harvard."

Certainly, that was said partly in jest. And if you read the remainder of the job description, you'd see that the tone of the ad was cheeky and clever, purposefully meant to indicate to job applicants what kind of company Chess.com is.

But by poking fun at the Harvard MBA, Chess.com is making a statement, and it's not about that university. The statement is that old-school rules no longer apply.

To lead their company, a successful candidate probably won't be defined by traditional criteria.

How could they be?

In 2014, the website said that more than a billion live games had been played on the site. In December 2022, Chess.com reached a milestone of 100 million users. In 2023, the website added AI bots.

Could a graduate from a business school that has graduated generations of corporate leaders be prepared to run a company like this? Yes, probably. But would that be a requirement?

Another sign is a recent post on Twitter, in which someone asked her followers a question: If someone's child got into Yale, which would require paying $40,000 a year, but also got a full scholarship for an honors biology program at their flagship state school in Florida, which would be the better option?

The answers were varied. Some expressed their belief that "brand is best."

"Yale," one Twitter follower responded. "The prestige and connections really do translate into better career and romantic prospects, as shallow and unfair as that may be."

"Yale," another follower echoed. "As elitist as it sounds, the networks that come out of Yale will be on a different level."

Others, however, emphasized the value of a degree from a credible state institution and the possibility of avoiding potentially decades' worth of debt.

"Definitely take the full ride," one follower said. "The debt will be way more harmful than that degree will be helpful."

"The full ride," another follower said. "It's been almost 20 years and my student loans have defined my life (still do) and I did NOT pay 40k (in tuition) a year."

One chimed in with solutions such as going to the state school for undergraduate and Yale for graduate. Another suggested spending the first two years at a school in state to save money, then to transfer to Yale.

And then there was this: "College counselor here," the follower said by means of introduction, "as long as cost is not an issue, the student should decide."

Good answer!

And the right one. College is a decision that *you* should make. Because when you set foot in your first university class, it's going to be your foot and no one else's.

So now that we've taken a bit of an inventory of the current situation when it comes to higher education, let's venture a bit ahead.

You're probably excited about going to college. And you should be.

But leaving the comfort of your home and family is a big step. It can feel incredibly exciting, like you're on the precipice of great change.

Maybe it's like you're on the high dive at your local pool, staring at the shimmering water below you. As you peer over the edge, it's the moment before you jump.

And, in many respects, right now, that's where you are.

Every high school graduate leaving the comfort of a campus and family knows that sensation. No more hanging out with friends in the cafeteria, varsity sport championship seasons, or proms. You may have convinced yourself that you were tired of all that, but the prospect of leaving all that behind might now be giving you pause.

People seem to reminisce about their own time in high school like those were their best and most carefree years, so that can add to how you're feeling right now.

And those months, if not years, researching university options and then preparing applications—that's all done. So now what lies ahead are the prospects of a new place, new courses, and new friends.

You might even be anticipating what happens after you graduate. Probably not that much, but enough so that you feel like what you do in college is going to count.

If it makes you feel any better, all the high school students who came before you felt the same way. That's natural. Feeling a bit nervous about what lies ahead is a good thing—that means that you care about what's in store.

It also means you're paying attention. Once you graduate from high school and head off to a university campus, you no longer can solely inhabit the comfortable bubble of home.

And that applies whether you're venturing an entire coast away from family or just commuting from your house. What's going on in the world around you will increasingly play a bigger role in your life.

What you hear about on the news or read about on the internet intersects more directly with what you are exposed to and what you do.

And sure, a lot of what's going on in the world can make you feel uneasy. There's certainly plenty going on—and not all of it good.

Political differences continue to polarize people in the United States. That will likely continue through your entire time at college and then beyond that.

There will likely be more protests about political issues, and that potentially involves students. And it's not just young people who worry about these problems. Adults worry as well.

You've probably heard about tension between the United States and countries like China. A great deal of that strain has to do with political differences as well as competition in key areas like technology. That will continue, too, through your college career.

And on top of that is climate change. Intensified hurricanes, typhoons, floods, and droughts will prevail throughout the country. If you move to another state to go to college, it's possible you'll notice changes in your immediate environment as well.

This is not to say that you need to get involved in any of this. But you'll feel like these events are closer and the urgency is more palpable.

It's fair to say that the challenges ahead are formidable—for all of us.

But at the same time, for every worrisome obstacle is an opportunity that could vault you even farther ahead than you can ever have imagined.

So what does your future look like?

It can look the way you want it to look!

To be fair, there are a few things you can't account for. Even if you're meticulous about what you study, networking as best you can, and getting great internships, things can go off the rails. As the saying goes, "The best-laid plans of mice and men often go awry."

This is derived from a line in the poem "To a Mouse" by Robert Burns. That means that even the most carefully thought-out and well-prepared plans can still fail or not go as expected. So don't be too hard on yourself if things don't exactly fall into place.

But aside from that, think big. Dream big. Don't sell yourself short.

There's another old saying: "Necessity is the mother of invention."

This phrase, attributed to the ancient Greek philosopher Plato, means that when there is a need or a problem to be solved, people are motivated to find creative solutions to address it. In other words, when people are faced with a difficult situation or a challenge, they are driven to come up with innovative ideas and solutions to overcome the obstacle.

There are many examples of this.

First, there's the wheel. The wheel was born out of a necessity to transport heavy loads more easily.

Then there's the printing press. Johannes Gutenberg's invention of the first mechanized printing press in the 15th century was driven by the need to produce books and other printed materials more efficiently and inexpensively.

And where would we be without the telephone? Alexander Graham Bell's invention was motivated by his desire to find a way for people to communicate with each other over long distances more easily.

Then there's penicillin. Sir Alexander Fleming's discovery of penicillin in 1928 was the result of a laboratory accident, but it was driven by the need for more effective ways to treat bacterial infections.

The history of human invention is full of examples of how necessity has driven innovation. This has led to the development of new technologies, products, and ideas that have improved our lives in countless ways.

But as we look into your future, how about turning that ol' saying on its head?

Invention is the mother of necessity.

You can have ideas that transform what people feel like they need.

A good example of that is Uber.

Before the ride-sharing company's launch in 2009, people had to make do with mass transit like trains and buses or taxis and their own cars. Hard to believe, right?

Today, Uber has millions of drivers across the globe and over 120 million active users. It also covers 10,000 towns and cities worldwide, according to some estimates.

Can you imagine your life without being able to call for an Uber (or a Lyft) on your phone and always needing to pay with cash or with a credit card at the end of your ride?

Or how about life without social media? Social media platforms like Facebook, Twitter, and Instagram were not originally developed out of necessity, but they have become an integral part of how many people communicate and share information with each other.

Back in the day, you'd have to pick up the phone or write a letter to stay in touch with a friend.

Other inventions that have become necessities are streaming services. Netflix and Spotify are not necessary for survival, but they have become a staple of modern entertainment.

Can you imagine having to wait to watch shows at specific times or buy an entire LP in order to listen to one song?

For you drivers out there, there's GPS navigation. GPS—or Global Positioning System—uses satellites to determine your location and time anywhere on Earth. It is commonly used for navigation, mapping, and timing purposes.

GPS was originally developed for military use, but it has become a ubiquitous part of modern life.

We can, of course, continue to use a paper map. But whether it's via a dedicated GPS device or a smartphone app, many of us rely on GPS to navigate our way around unfamiliar places.

And finally, but certainly not least, is online shopping. We could drive to the mall and shop in brick-and-mortar stores. But online shopping lets us buy clothes and consumer goods from all over the world without leaving our homes.

Overall, many modern innovations that were not originally developed out of necessity have become essential parts of our daily lives. They have become so firmly embedded in our everyday routines that we can't imagine life without them.

So that's why you should consider yourself lucky to be graduating during these transformational times. If innovative ideas can quickly become essential aspects of our existence, the upside to your own life is truly limitless.

Of course, there are many unknowns, especially as tech, AI, and machine learning disrupt and uproot industries right and left.

But with challenges come opportunities. And they will be plentiful for those who are ready for them.

In this book, we've talked a lot about making decisions to maximize your college experience. And if you've been true to yourself, by the time you graduate, you'll probably have a pretty good idea about what you might want to do.

But even if you don't, you will have the skills and competencies that can lead down many pathways.

There's nothing wrong with going down a few wrong avenues.

Remember that Shopify originated as a snowboard company.[2] Shopify founder Tobias Lütke started an online snowboard shop but soon discovered that there was more interest in the software he had written to power his online store than in the snowboards.

YouTube was originally a dating site, with cofounder Steve Chen initially believing the site would be a platform for people to upload videos of themselves to find romantic partners.[3]

Instagram was a whiskey app, with cofounder Kevin Systrom creating a location-based iPhone app initially designed to let users check in at particular locations to make plans and post pictures of meet-ups with other whiskey lovers.[4] He soon found out the app's photo-sharing feature was what was popular, whiskey notwithstanding.

And finally, streaming giant Netflix was once a decidedly low-tech DVD-mailing service, with *Beetlejuice* being the first DVD to be shipped out in 1998, starring Winona Ryder (who would later appear in Netflix's hit *Stranger Things*).[5]

It may be about being first, but more important, it is about getting started.

Make no mistake about it—there are famous universities that will continue to reign supreme on the higher-education landscape. Getting an education from an elite institution will remain a privilege, and the prospect of gaining that competitive edge will propel more and more students to apply to Ivy League schools and rankings-adjacent compatriots.

But there are more opportunities than ever for university students to catch that brass ring. A bright future is in sight for all—and flickers most brilliantly for those who know how to attain it.

You are navigating a complex educational path within a world rife with challenges and anxiety. However, young people—*like you!*—are more inclined to search for individual meaning and willing to question the status quo. So forge ahead with confidence and excitement. Make college your superpower.

Readers of this book will have an ear to the ground, ready for the rumbling they hear in the distance to become a resounding roar.

And you'll be at the forefront of a transformation, with a starring role in what the world will become.

DECISION
NAVIGATOR

*G*et started!
If you're having a hard time organizing your thoughts, here's a simple checklist to work through.

Look at it this way: you're on a thrilling quest to unlock the secret to what truly matters to you. It's like finding the ultimate cheat code for personal success.

Start from the top and navigate your way down:

1. What are your career interests and goals?
   - Consider what subjects or fields you like.
   - Imagine your best life 10 years from now.
2. What are you good at?
   - Think not only of school but of your life as well.
   - Identify areas where you excel and where you need improvement.
3. Where do you want to live?
   - Decide whether you prefer studying close to home or in a different city or even country.
   - Consider factors such as climate, lifestyle, and proximity to family.

4. Which school has what you want?
   - Determine which universities/colleges offer programs aligned with your goals.
   - Look for institutions with a strong reputation in your chosen field.
5. What's fun for you?
   - Research the social atmosphere of each institution.
   - Explore clubs, organizations, and extracurricular activities that align with your interests.
6. What can you afford?
   - Consider tuition fees and available scholarships or financial aid options.
   - Assess the cost of living in different locations.
7. Go take a look!
   - Schedule visits to the shortlisted universities/colleges.
   - Attend open houses or information sessions to get a feel for the campus environment.
8. Ask for help.
   - Consult your high school counselors or teachers for guidance.
   - Ask an adult (not your parents) who you trust and admire for their input.
9. Follow your gut.
   - Reflect on your intuitions about each institution.
   - Trust your instincts and choose a university/college that feels right for you.

This is just a guide. How you weigh each factor may vary depending on your individual circumstances and priorities. Take your time, conduct thorough research, and make an informed choice based on you—not on them. Good luck with your decision!

NOTES

INTRODUCTION

1. Robby, "Cornell University: 2023 Requirements, Scores & GPAs," *Education Today*, April 3, 2023, https://educationtodaynews.net/cornell-university-acceptance-rate-gpa (June 15, 2023).

2. "Cost to Attend | Financial Aid," *Cornell University*, n.d., https://finaid.cornell.edu/cost-attend (June 15, 2023).

3. John Freeman Gill, "Restoring Brooklyn's Queen of Department Stores," *New York Times*, November 22, 2019, https://www.nytimes.com/2019/11/22/realestate/restoring-brooklyns-queen-of-department-stores.html (June 15, 2023).

CHAPTER 1

1. Jaison R. Abel and Richard Deitz, "Despite Rising Costs, College Is Still a Good Investment," *Liberty Street Economics*, June 16, 2021, https://libertystreeteconomics.newyorkfed.org/2019/06/despite-rising-costs-college-is-still-a-good-investment (June 5, 2023).

2. "A Brief History of New York University," *New York University Web Communications*, n.d., https://www.nyu.edu/faculty/governance-policies-and

-procedures/faculty-handbook/the-university/history-and-traditions-of-new
-york-university/a-brief-history-of-new-york-university.html (June 13, 2023).

3. Evan Hecht, "What Years Are Gen X? A Detailed Breakdown of When
Each Generation Was Born," *USA Today*, May 9, 2023, https://www.usatoday
.com/story/news/2022/09/02/what-years-gen-x-millennials-baby-boomers-gen
-z/10303085002 (June 6, 2023).

4. Richard Fry, "Millennials Outnumbered Boomers in 2019," *Pew Research
Center*, May 22, 2023, https://www.pewresearch.org/fact-tank/2020/04/28/mil
lennials-overtake-baby-boomers-as-americas-largest-generation (June 6, 2023).

5. "A Brief History of New York University."

6. Arnav Binaykia, "NYU Acceptance Rate Drops to 8% for Class of
2027," *Washington Square News*, March 28, 2023, https://nyunews.com/news
/2023/03/29/nyu-admission-rate-class-of-2027 (June 14, 2023).

7. Valerie J. Macmillan, "Acceptance Rate Is Lowest of Ivies," *Harvard Crimson*, April 12, 1995, https://www.thecrimson.com/article/1995/4/12
/acceptance-rate-is-lowest-of-ivies/#:~:text=The%20record%2011.8%20per
cent%20admission,14%20percent%20of%20its%20applicants (June 3, 2023).

8. Michelle N. Amponsah and Emma H. Haidar, "Harvard College Accepts
3.41% of Applicants to Class of 2027," *Harvard Crimson*, March 31, 2023,
https://www.thecrimson.com/article/2023/3/31/admissions-decisions-2027
(June 3, 2023).

9. Yi-Jin Yu, "High Schooler Accepted into 72 Colleges Shares Advice
for Other Students," *Good Morning America*, April 27, 2022, https://www
.goodmorningamerica.com/living/story/high-schooler-accepted-72-colleges
-shares-advice-students-84325285#:~:text=Ja'Leaha%20Thornton%20of%20
Belle,from%2072%20schools%20and%20counting (June 4, 2023).

10. Ezekiel J. Walker, "ATL Teen Accepted by 50+ Colleges with $1.3
Million in Scholarships," *Black Wall Street Times*, March 15, 2023, https://
theblackwallsttimes.com/2023/03/15/atl-teen-accepted-by-50-colleges-with
-1-3-million-in-scholarships (June 4, 2023).

11. Adisa Hargett-Robinson, "Florida Teen Accepted into 27 Universities with $4 Million in Scholarships," *Good Morning America*, April 13, 2022,
https://www.goodmorningamerica.com/living/story/florida-teen-accepted
-27-universities-million-scholarships-84030228 (June 3, 2023).

12. Ricardo Vazquez, "UCLA Applications for Fall 2023 Admission Remain
at Near-Historic Highs," *UCLA*, February 24, 2023, https://newsroom.ucla.edu

/releases/ucla-applications-for-fall-2023-admissions#:~:text=Freshman%20ap
plications%20dipped%202.6%25%20from,strong%20and%20unchanged%20
from%202022 (June 4, 2023).

13. Joe Vigil, "Southern Nevada Has 8 Years of Water Reserves as State
Faces Water Cuts from Colorado River," *Fox 5*, August 20, 2022, https://www
.fox5vegas.com/2022/08/20/southern-nevada-has-eight-years-water-reserves
-nevada-faces-water-shortage-cuts-colorado-river (June 13, 2023).

14. Julia Jacobo, "Coral Reefs Could Stop Growing in 10 Years unless
Greenhouse Gases Are Significantly Reduced, New Study Says," *ABC News*,
May 11, 2021, https://abcnews.go.com/International/coral-reefs-stop-growing
-80-years-greenhouse-gases/story?id=77532016 (June 13, 2023).

15. Klaus Dodds, "Skiing in the Alps Faces a Bleak Future Thanks to Climate Change," *Phys.Org*, December 31, 2022, https://phys.org/news/2022-12
-alps-bleak-future-climate.html (June 5, 2023).

16. Laurie Goering, "Solar-Power Internet Downloads Opportunities for
African Refugees," *Reuters*, November 17, 2022, https://www.reuters.com
/business/cop/solar-power-internet-downloads-opportunities-african-refu
gees-2022-11-17 (June 12, 2023)

17. "Quote of the Day Archives," *Wheaton College*, n.d., https://www.wheaton
.edu/life-at-wheaton/kingdom-diversity/quote-of-the-day-archives (June 5,
2023).

18. "Barack Obama's Feb. 5 Speech," *New York Times*, February 6, 2008,
https://www.nytimes.com/2008/02/05/us/politics/05text-obama.html%20
(June 6, 2023).

CHAPTER 2

1. Robert Morse and Eric Brooks, "A More Detailed Look at the Ranking Factors," *U.S. News & World Report*, September 12, 2022, https://
www.usnews.com/education/best-colleges/articles/ranking-criteria-and
-weights#:~:text=To%20most%20accurately%20represent%20the,effect%20
on%20that%20school's%20ranking (June 6, 2023).

2. "Harvard Admits 3.4% of Students to the Class of 2027," *Crimson
Education*, n.d., https://www.crimsoneducation.org/us/blog/admissions-news
/harvard-acceptance-rate (June 3, 2023).

3. John S. Rosenberg, "Harvard Admits Record-Low 5.2 Percent of Applicants to Class of 2020," *Harvard Magazine*, April 1, 2016, https://www.harvardmagazine.com/2016/04/harvard-accepts-record-low-5-2-percent-of-applicants-to-class-of-2020#:~:text=Harvard%20Admits%20Record%2DLow%205.2%20Percent%20of%20Applicants%20to%20Class%20of%202020&text=Harvard%20College%20announced%20today%20that,granted%20early%2Daction%20admission (June 5, 2023).

4. Michelle N. Amponsah and Emma H. Haidar, "Harvard College Accepts 3.41% of Applicants to Class of 2027," *Harvard Crimson*, March 31, 2023, https://www.thecrimson.com/article/2023/3/31/admissions-decisions-2027 (June 3, 2023).

5. David Curran, "UC Acceptance Rates 1997–2017," *SFGATE*, April 11, 2018, https://www.sfgate.com/news/slideshow/UC-acceptance-rates-1997-2017-179965.php (June 3, 2023).

6. Teresa Watanabe, "UC Applications Slow Down for Fall 2023 with Drop in Out-of-State Students," *Los Angeles Times*, February 24, 2023, https://www.latimes.com/california/story/2023-02-24/uc-applications-slow-down-for-fall-2023-with-drop-in-out-of-state-students (June 4, 2023).

7. Janet Gilmore, "UC Berkeley Sees Record Number of Freshman Applications," *UC Berkeley News Archive*, April 5, 2007, https://newsarchive.berkeley.edu/news/media/releases/2007/04/05_admissions.shtml#:~:text=Although%20the%20number%20of%20individual,from%2023.6%20in%20fall%202006 (June 5, 2023).

8. David Curran, "UC Acceptance Rates 1997–2017," *SFGATE*, March 29, 2018, https://www.sfgate.com/news/slideshow/UC-acceptance-rates-1997-2017-179965.php (June 5, 2023).

9. "Freshman Admit Data | UC Admissions," *University of California*, n.d., https://admission.universityofcalifornia.edu/campuses-majors/berkeley/freshman-admit-data.html (June 6, 2023).

10. Sarah Wood, "Colleges with the Highest Application Fees," *U.S. News & World Report*, January 28, 2022, https://www.usnews.com/education/best-colleges/the-short-list-college/articles/colleges-with-the-highest-application-fees (June 13, 2023).

11. Shawn M. Carter, "Colleges Make a Fortune from Saying 'No' to Applications—Here's How Much," *CNBC*, September 28, 2017, https://www

.cnbc.com/2017/09/28/how-much-money-colleges-make-rejecting-students -applications.html (June 13, 2023).

12. Jeffrey Selingo, "The Cynical Reason College Applications Are Surging," *New York Times*, March 16, 2023, https://www.nytimes.com/2023/03/16 /opinion/college-admissions-common-app.html (June 20, 2023).

13. Mike Brown, "Which U.S. Colleges Make the Most Revenue from Applications?," *LendEDU*, April 6, 2023, https://lendedu.com/blog/which-colleges -make-most-revenue-from-applications (June 13, 2023).

14. Josh Moody, "Colleges That Received the Most Applications," *U.S. News & World Report*, October 19, 2021, https://www.usnews.com/educa tion/best-colleges/the-short-list-college/articles/colleges-that-received-the-most -applications (July 3, 2023).

15. Anna Esaki-Smith, "Yale Law School Withdraws from U.S. News Rankings over Methodology," *Forbes*, November 16, 2022, https://www.forbes.com /sites/annaesakismith/2022/11/16/yale-law-school-withdraws-from-us-news -rankings-over-methodology/?sh=7fb48d0726c7 (June 13, 2023).

16. Laura M. Schacter, "Race, Criminal Justice, and Migration Control: Enforcing the Boundaries of Belonging," *Michigan Law Review* 115, no. 8 (June 2017): 1315–70, https://repository.law.umich.edu/cgi/viewcontent.cgi ?params=/context/mlr/article/5435/&path_info= (June 13, 2023).

17. John Smith, "Columbia University Drops in U.S. News Rankings," *New York Times*, June 6, 2023, https://www.nytimes.com/2023/06/06/us/columbia -university-us-news-rankings.html (July 8, 2023).

18. "CSU San Marcos Tops Ninth Annual Social Mobility Index of Schools Driving the American Dream through Their Ethos and Action," *Businesswire.com*, November 4, 2022, https://www.businesswire.com/news/home /20221104005031/en (June 14, 2023).

19. Lotte van Rijswijk, "The Happiest Schools in the U.S., UK and Australia," *Resume.io*, March 22, 2023, https://resume.io/blog/the-happiest-schools -in-the-us-uk-and-australia (June 14, 2023).

20. Benjamin Wermund, "How U.S. News College Rankings Promote Economic Inequality on Campus," *Politico*, September 10, 2017, https://www .politico.com/interactives/2017/top-college-rankings-list-2017-us-news-investi gation (June 13, 2023).

21. "2019 State of College Admission Report," *National Association for College Admission Counseling*, May 15, 2023, https://www.nacacnet.org/2019-state-of-college-admission-report (June 15, 2023).

22. "Fast Facts: Enrollment (98)," *National Center for Education Statistics*, n.d., https://nces.ed.gov/fastfacts/display.asp?id=98 (June 15, 2023).

23. "SOC2019: State of College Admission," *National Association for College Admission Counseling*, https://nacacnet.org/wp-content/uploads/2022/10/soca2019_all.pdf (June 16, 2023).

24. Douglas Belkin, "For Sale: SAT Takers' Names. Colleges Buy Student Data and Boost Exclusivity," *Wall Street Journal*, November 5, 2019, https://www.wsj.com/articles/for-sale-sat-takers-names-colleges-buy-student-data-and-boost-exclusivity-11572976621 (June 13, 2023).

25. Alina Tugend, "Who Benefits from the Expansion of AP Classes?," *New York Times*, September 7, 2017, https://www.nytimes.com/2017/09/07/magazine/who-benefits-from-the-expansion-of-ap-classes.html (July 5, 2023).

26. Ryan Glasspiegel, "Shohei Ohtani Gave Rousing World Baseball Classic Speech to Team Japan," *New York Post*, March 22, 2023, https://nypost.com/2023/03/21/shohei-ohtani-rallies-japan-with-pre-wbc-final-speech (July 2, 2023).

CHAPTER 3

1. Yue Wang, "Alibaba Loses $21 Billion In Market Value After Suspending Cloud Unit IPO And Jack Ma Sells Shares," Forbes, November 17, 2023, https://www.forbes.com/sites/ywang/2023/11/17/alibaba-loses-21-billion-in-market-value-after-suspending-cloud-unit-ipo-and-jack-ma-sells-shares/?sh=12c6ff854c70 (December 21, 2023).

2. C. Custer, "Connecting Asia's Startup Ecosystem," *Tech in Asia*, May 14, 2015, https://www.techinasia.com/jack-ma-what-told-son-education (June 8, 2023).

3. Alp Mimaroglu, "How Jack Ma Overcame His 7 Biggest Failures," *Entrepreneur*, September 9, 2016, https://www.entrepreneur.com/leadership/how-jack-ma-overcame-his-7-biggest-failures/275969 (June 9, 2023).

4. Neil Gough and Alexandra Stevenson, "The Unlikely Ascent of Jack Ma, Alibaba's Founder," *New York Times*, May 7, 2014, https://www.nytimes

.com/2014/05/08/technology/the-unlikely-ascent-of-jack-ma-alibabas-founder
.html (June 8, 2023).

5. Lulu Yilun Chen, "Alibaba," *Bloomberg.com*, November 20, 2017, https://www.bloomberg.com/quicktake/alibaba#xj4y7vzkg (June 9, 2023).

6. Ryan Browne, "Alibaba sheds over $20 billion in market value after scrapping plans to list its cloud business," CNBC, November 17, 2023, https://www.cnbc.com/2023/11/17/alibaba-sheds-20-billion-in-market-cap-as-cloud-spinoff-scrapped.html (December 21, 2023).

7. Kerry A. Dolan, "Forbes' 35th Annual World's Billionaires List: Facts and Figures 2021," *Forbes*, April 6, 2021, https://www.forbes.com/sites/kerryadolan/2021/04/06/forbes-35th-annual-worlds-billionaires-list-facts-and-figures-2021/?sh=61a4ca885e58 (June 13, 2023).

8. "The Best Universities in China, Ranked," *U.S. News & World Report*, n.d., https://www.usnews.com/education/best-global-universities/china?city=hangzhou (June 8, 2023).

9. "Jack Ma: Don't Try to Be the Best, Be the First!," *YouTube*, n.d., https://www.youtube.com/watch?v=Uiztg_i0P9g (June 13, 2023).

10. "10 Facts about Today's College Graduates," *Pew Research Center*, n.d., https://www.pewresearch.org/short-reads/2022/04/12/10-facts-about-todays-college-graduates (June 13, 2023).

11. "Combination of Artificial Intelligence and Radiologists More Accurately Identified Breast Cancer," *NYU Langone Health*, October 17, 2019, https://www.nyu.edu/about/news-publications/news/2019/october/combination-of-artificial-intelligence---radiologists-more-accur.html (June 13, 2023).

12. Alice Park, "Google's AI Will Now Be Used in Mammograms," *Time*, November 28, 2022, https://time.com/6237088/mammograms-google-ai (June 13, 2023).

13. "Can Artificial Intelligence Perfect Mammography?," *NYU Langone Health*, n.d., https://nyulangone.org/news/can-artificial-intelligence-perfect-mammography (June 13, 2023).

14. "Noel Quinn," *HSBC Holdings Plc*, n.d., https://www.hsbc.com/who-we-are/leadership-and-governance/board-of-directors/noel-quinn (June 13, 2023).

15. "History Timeline," *HSBC Holdings Plc*, n.d., https://www.hsbc.com/who-we-are/our-history/history-timeline (June 13, 2023).

16. Simon Clark and Margot Patrick, "HSBC Appoints Noel Quinn as Permanent CEO," *Wall Street Journal*, March 17, 2020, https://www.wsj.com /articles/hsbc-appoints-noel-quinn-as-permanent-ceo-11584469873 (June 13, 2023).

17. Lauren Motzkin, "Expenses a Concern for Arts Majors," *Yale Daily News*, November 10, 2012, https://yaledailynews.com/blog/2009/11/20/ex penses-a-concern-for-arts-majors (June 15, 2023).

18. Christal Young, "Museum of Failure Exhibit Opens in Brooklyn," *Fox 5 New York*, April 1, 2023, https://www.fox5ny.com/news/museum-of-failure -nyc-brooklyn-open-march-may-14 (June 16, 2023).

CHAPTER 4

1. "All Tony Awards Won by Carnegie Mellon University Faculty, Students and Alumni," *Carnegie Mellon University*, n.d., https://www.cmu.edu/about /awards.html#AllTonyAwards (June 13, 2023).

2. "Carnegie Mellon to Become First Exclusive Higher Education Partner of the Tony Awards," *Tony Awards*, n.d., https://www.tonyawards.com/press /carnegie-mellon-to-become-first-exclusive-higher-education-partner-of-the -tony-awards (June 13, 2023).

3. Mike Winters, "The 10 Highest-Paying College Majors, Five Years after Graduation," *CNBC*, February 20, 2023, https://www.cnbc.com/2023/02/20 /highest-paying-college-majors.html (June 13, 2023).

4. Emily Krutsch and Victoria Roderick, "STEM Day: Explore Growing Careers," *U.S. Department of Labor Blog*, November 4, 2022, https:// blog.dol.gov/2022/11/04/stem-day-explore-growing-careers#:~:text=In %202021%2C%20there%20were%20nearly%2010%20million%20 workers,STEM%20occupations%2C%20compared%20to%20 %2440%2C120%20for%20non-STEM%20occupations (June 13, 2023).

5. Victoria Masterson, "These Are the Degrees That Will Earn You the Most Money When You Graduate—and the Ones That Won't," *World Economic Forum*, October 28, 2021, https://www.weforum.org/agenda/2021/10/stem -degrees-most-valuable/#:~:text=The%20top%2025%20college%20 degrees%20by%20pay%20and,least%20valuable%20degrees%2C%20with%20 average%20pay%20of%20%2435%2C500 (June 13, 2023).

6. Quoctrung Bui, "How 'Build Your Own College Rankings' Was Built," *New York Times*, March 27, 2023, https://www.nytimes.com/2023/03/27/opinion/how-build-your-own-college-rankings-was-built.html (June 13, 2023).

7. "The Best Universities in the World, Ranked," *U.S. News & World Report*, n.d., https://www.usnews.com/education/best-global-universities/rankings (June 9, 2023).

8. Winters, "The Worst Paying College Majors, Five Years After Graduation."

9. Hamilton, "Digital #Ham4Ham 1/17/16—'Martin Luther King,' Words & Music by Barbara Ames," *YouTube*, January 17, 2016, https://www.youtube.com/watch?v=7EITcerK6kM (June 13, 2023).

10. Staff Reporter, "John Legend: My Success Is Due to the Teachers Who Believed in Me," *HuffPost UK* (blog), November 8, 2017, https://www.huffingtonpost.co.uk/entry/level-playing-field-for-students_uk_5c7e9943e4b048b41e3a2d99 (June 13, 2023).

11. "Jon Hamm 'Might Still' Go Back to Teaching—and He Has a Name for the Class," *Today*, January 20, 2023, https://www.today.com/video/jon-hamm-might-still-go-back-to-teaching-and-he-has-a-name-for-the-class-957938755685 (June 13, 2023).

12. Anna Watson, "Ranking the Top Schools for a Career in Marketing," *Poets&Quants for Undergrads*, April 2, 2023, https://poetsandquantsforundergrads.com/uncategorized/ranking-the-top-schools-for-a-career-in-marketing/#:~:text=The%20University%20of%20Wisconsin%20at,new%20ranking%20from%20BookYourData.com (June 13, 2023).

13. "US News Best Colleges," *U.S. News & World Report*, n.d., https://www.usnews.com/best-colleges (June 10, 2023).

14. Barry Schwartz, *The Paradox of Choice: Why More Is Less*, 2004, https://changethis.com/manifesto/13.ParadoxOfChoice/pdf/13.ParadoxOfChoice.pdf (June 13, 2023).

CHAPTER 5

1. Joanna York, "Does Doing What You Love for a Living Come with a Price?," *BBC Worklife*, February 25, 2022, https://www.bbc.com/worklife/article/20210927-does-doing-what-you-love-for-a-living-come-with-a-price (June 13, 2023).

2. Angela Bailey, "CHCO Blog—Light the Fire within You," *Department of Homeland Security*, February 3, 2021, https://www.dhs.gov/employee-resources/blog/2021/02/03/chco-blog-light-fire-within-you (June 13, 2023).

3. "Ariana Grande Quotes," *Goodreads*, https://www.goodreads.com/quotes/search?q=Ariana+grande (June 13, 2023).

4. "Oprah Winfrey: Passion Is Energy," *Bloomberg*, October 15, 2015, https://www.bloomberg.com/news/videos/2015-10-15/oprah-winfrey-passion-is-energy (June 16, 2023).

5. Lex Clips, "Steve Jobs: The Only Way to Do Great Work Is to Love What You Do," December 25, 2019, https://www.youtube.com/watch?v=JV3OqaRmBk4 (June 14, 2023).

6. "Average Vogue Salary: By Location, Job Title, and Department," *Zippia*, August 22, 2022, https://www.zippia.com/vogue-careers-68033/salary (June 15, 2023).

7. "Assistant to the Editor-in-Chief, American Vogue and Global Chief Content Officer at Condé Nast," *LinkedIn*, https://www.linkedin.com/jobs/view/assistant-to-the-editor-in-chief-american-vogue-and-global-chief-content-officer-at-cond%C3%A9-nast-3633023278 (July 8, 2023).

8. Anna Bahney, "Manhattan Median Rents Hit Another High in March," *CNN Business*, April 13, 2023, https://edition.cnn.com/2023/04/13/homes/manhattan-rentals-march/index.html (June 13, 2023).

9. Mary K. Jacob, "Manhattan Rents Reach All-Time High at $4,175 per Month as Exodus Continues," *New York Post*, April 13, 2023, https://nypost.com/2023/04/13/manhattan-median-rents-reach-an-all-time-high-of-4175-month (June 15, 2023).

10. Jessica Dickler, "Scrub Daddy CEO Credits College for His Clean Start," *CNBC*, June 26, 2017, https://www.cnbc.com/2017/06/23/scrub-daddy-ceo-credits-college-for-his-start-in-the-sponge-business.html (June 14, 2023).

11. Holly Johnson, "Scrub Daddy: The Story behind Shark Tank US's Biggest Success," *CEO Magazine*, February 8, 2019, https://www.theceomagazine.com/business/innovation-technology/scrub-daddy-the-story-behind-shark-tank-uss-biggest-success (June 15, 2023).

12. Gillian Zoe Segal, "This Self-Made Billionaire Failed the LSAT Twice, Then Sold Fax Machines for 7 Years before Hitting Big—Here's How She Got There," *CNBC*, April 3, 2019, https://www.cnbc.com/2019/04/03/self-made

-billionaire-spanx-founder-sara-blakely-sold-fax-machines-before-making-it -big.html (June 12, 2023).

13. Alexandra Alter and Elizabeth A. Harris, "What Snoop Dogg's Success Says about the Book Industry," *New York Times*, April 28, 2021, https://www .nytimes.com/2021/04/18/books/book-sales-publishing-pandemic-coronavirus .html (June 11, 2023).

14. "Colleges with Great Writing Programs," *U.S. News & World Report*, n.d., https://www.usnews.com/best-colleges/rankings/writing-programs (June 10, 2023).

15. Derek Saul, "NBA Docks Mavericks $750,000 for Tanking—Just .01% of Billionaire Owner Mark Cuban's Net Worth," *Forbes*, April 14, 2023, https://www.forbes.com/sites/dereksaul/2023/04/14/nba-docks-mavericks -750000-for-tanking-just-0001-of-billionaire-owner-mark-cubans-net-worth /?sh=347362296f0f (June 16, 2023).

16. Catherine Clifford, "Billionaire Mark Cuban: 'One of the Great Lies of Life Is Follow Your Passions,'" *CNBC*, November 13, 2020, https:// www.cnbc.com/2018/02/16/mark-cuban-follow-your-passion-is-bad-advice .html#:~:text=%E2%80%9COne%20of%20the%20great%20lies%20of%20 life%20is%20'follow%20your,what%20you%20are%20passionate%20about (June 14, 2023).

17. Catherine Clifford, "Jeff Bezos: You Can't Pick Your Passions," *CNBC*, February 7, 2019, https://www.cnbc.com/2019/02/07/amazon-and-blue-origins -jeff-bezos-on-identifying-your-passion.html (June 13, 2023).

18. "Academic Calendar," *UCLA Registrar's Office*, n.d., https://registrar .ucla.edu/file/10daf248-1afe-4043-a5c2-72cabc547221 (June 13, 2023).

19. Anna Esaki-Smith, "US Renews Commitment to International Students and Presence on 'World Stage,'" *Forbes*, July 27, 2021, https://www.forbes .com/sites/annaesakismith/2021/07/26/us-renews-commitment-to-international -students-and-presence-on-world-stage/?sh=451382704236 (June 13, 2023).

20. "OES Home," *U.S. Bureau of Labor Statistics*, April 25, 2023, https:// www.bls.gov/oes/#:~:text=The%20Occupational%20Employment%20and%20 Wage,annually%20for%20approximately%20830%20occupations (June 15, 2023).

21. "Google Entry Level Software Engineer Salaries," *Glassdoor*, n.d., https://www.glassdoor.com/Salary/Google-Entry-Level-Software-Engineer -Salaries-E9079_D_KO7,36.htm (June 10, 2023).

22. "Salary: Entry-Level Reporter in United States June 2023," *Glassdoor*, n.d., https://www.glassdoor.com/Salaries/entry-level-reporter-salary-SRCH _KO0,20.htm (June 10, 2023).

23. Catherine Clifford, "Jeff Bezos Says This Is How He Plans to Spend the Bulk of His Fortune," *CNBC*, April 30, 2018, https://www.cnbc.com/2018 /04/30/jeff-bezos-says-this-is-how-he-plans-to-spend-the-bulk-of-his-for tune.html#:~:text=Bezos%20says%20his%20work%20on%20Blue%20 Origin%2C%20his,continue%20to%20do%20that%20for%20a%20long%20 time (June 14, 2023).

24. "The Top Ten Richest People in the World," *Forbes*, June 1, 2023, https://www.forbes.com/sites/forbeswealthteam/article/the-top-ten-richest-peo ple-in-the-world/?sh=704792e354dc (June 13, 2023).

25. Jamie Carter, "Jeff Bezos' Blue Origin Bags New NASA Contract for Mars Mission," *Forbes*, February 10, 2023, https://www.forbes.com/sites /jamiecartereurope/2023/02/10/jeff-bezos-blue-origin-bags-new-nasa-contract -for-mars-mission/?sh=51fc93fd2015 (June 14, 2023).

CHAPTER 6

1. Jean Twenge, Wendy Wang, Jenet Erickson, and Brad Wilcox, "Teens and Tech 2022, What Difference Does Family Structure Make?" *Institute for Family Studies*, October 2022, https://ifstudies.org/reports/teens-and-tech /2022/executive-summary (June 10, 2023).

2. CyberSeek, "Cybersecurity Remains One of the Most in Demand Profes-sions, New Data from CyberSeek Confirms," *PR Newswire*, October 17, 2022, https://www.prnewswire.com/news-releases/cybersecurity-remains-one-of-the -most-in-demand-professions-new-data-from-cyberseek-confirms-301651014 .html (June 10, 2023).

3. CyberSeek, "Cybersecurity Remains One of the Most In-Demand Professions."

4. David Ng, "Obama Shows His Support for National Arts and Humanities Month," *Los Angeles Times*, October 4, 2010, https://www.latimes.com/archives /blogs/culture-monster-blog/story/2010-10-04/obama-shows-his-support-for -national-arts-and-humanities-month#:~:text=A%20PROCLAMATION%20 Throughout%20history%2C%20the%20arts%20and%20humanities,us%20

and%20reminding%20us%20of%20our%20shared%20humanity (June 13, 2023).

5. Jill Barshay, "PROOF POINTS: The Number of College Graduates in the Humanities Drops for the Eighth Consecutive Year," *The Hechinger Report*, November 23, 2021, https://hechingerreport.org/proof-points-the-number -of-college-graduates-in-the-humanities-drops-for-the-eighth-consecutive-year (June 14, 2023).

6. Barshay, "PROOF POINTS."

7. "Current Term Enrollment Estimates," *National Student Clearinghouse Research Center*, May 24, 2023, https://nscresearchcenter.org/current-term -enrollment-estimates (June 10, 2023).

8. Dana Wilkie, "Employers Say Students Aren't Learning Soft Skills in College," *Society for Human Resource Management*, October 21, 2019, https:// www.shrm.org/resourcesandtools/hr-topics/employee-relations/pages/employ ers-say-students-arent-learning-soft-skills-in-college.aspx (June 13, 2023).

9. Wilkie, "Employers Say Students Aren't Learning Soft Skills in College."

10. Wilkie, "Employers Say Students Aren't Learning Soft Skills in College."

11. Shayna Waltower, "The Skills Gap Is Costing Businesses Dearly," *Business News Daily*, February 21, 2023, https://www.businessnewsdaily.com /6038-skills-gaps-cost-companies-thousands.html (June 14, 2023).

12. CareerBuilder Hiring Solutions, "The Skills Gap Is Costing Companies Nearly $1 Million Annually, according to New CareerBuilder Survey," *Press Room, Career Builder*, April 13, 2017, https://press.careerbuilder.com/2017 -04-13-The-Skills-Gap-is-Costing-Companies-Nearly-1-Million-Annually -According-to-New-CareerBuilder-Survey#:~:text=According%20to%20a%20 new%20CareerBuilder,is%20more%20than%20%24800%2C000%20annually (June 15, 2023).

13. Dana Goldstein and Stephanie Saul. "College Board Will Change Its AP African American Studies Course," *New York Times*, April 25, 2023, https:// www.nytimes.com/2023/04/24/us/ap-african-american-studies-college-board .html (June 15, 2023).

14. Ileana Najarro, "States Are Mandating Asian American Studies. What Should the Curriculum Look Like?," *Education Week*, November 29, 2022, https://www.edweek.org/teaching-learning/states-are-mandating-asian-ameri can-studies-what-should-the-curriculum-look-like/2022/10 (June 13, 2023).

15. Nikki Brahm, "Experts Call for Increased Asian American Studies to Counter Ignorance and Hate," *INSIGHT Into Diversity*, May 20, 2023, https://www.insightintodiversity.com/experts-call-for-increased-asian-american-studies-to-counter-ignorance-and-hate (June 16, 2023).

16. George Anders, "Who's Vaulting into the C-Suite? Trends Changed Fast in 2022," *LinkedIn*, February 1, 2023, https://www.linkedin.com/pulse/whos-vaulting-c-suite-trends-changed-fast-2022-george-anders (June 10, 2023).

17. "State of the Humanities 2021: Workforce & Beyond," *American Academy of Arts & Sciences*, March 10, 2023, https://www.amacad.org/publication/humanities-workforce-beyond (June 11, 2023).

CHAPTER 7

1. Melanie Hanson, "Average Cost of College [2023]: Yearly Tuition + Expenses," *Education Data Initiative*, May 18, 2023, https://educationdata.org/average-cost-of-college (June 20, 2023).

2. Hanson, "Average Cost of College [2023]."

3. "Tuition and Fees," *Amherst College*, n.d., https://www.amherst.edu/tuition (June 20, 2023).

4. "Cost of Attendance," *Harvey Mudd College*, n.d., https://www.hmc.edu/admission/afford/cost-of-attendance (June 19, 2023).

5. "Cost & Affordability," *Columbia Undergraduate Admissions*, n.d., https://undergrad.admissions.columbia.edu/affordability/cost (June 20, 2023).

6. Pete D'Amato, "University of Chicago Projected to Be the First U.S. University to Charge $100,000 a Year," *Hechinger Report*, October 30, 2019, https://hechingerreport.org/university-of-chicago-projected-to-be-the-first-u-s-university-to-charge-100000-a-year (June 20, 2023).

7. "Chicago Housing Market," *Redfin*, n.d., https://www.redfin.com/city/29470/IL/Chicago/housing-market (June 14, 2023).

8. Jeff Manning, "Phil Knight's University of Oregon Donations Push $1 Billion Mark with New Hayward Field Project," *Oregonlive*, March 9, 2021, https://www.oregonlive.com/news/2021/03/knights-university-of-oregon-donations-push-1-billion-mark-with-new-hayward-field-project.html (June 14, 2023).

9. "Portland State Athletics Unveils New Logo and Branding," *Portland State University Athletics*, May 19, 2016, https://goviks.com/news/2016/5/19/portland-state-athletics-with-help-from-nike-unveils-new-logo-and-branding.aspx#:~:text=Portland%20State%20University%2C%20in%20partnership,PSU%20Athletic%20Director%20Mark%20Rountree%20 (June 14, 2023).

10. Alison Green, "Why Employers Don't Like Long-Distance Job Candidates," *U.S. News & World Report*, July 7, 2014, https://money.usnews.com/money/blogs/outside-voices-careers/2014/07/07/why-employers-dont-like-long-distance-job-candidates (June 16, 2023).

11. "Partnerships," *Embry-Riddle Aeronautical University*, n.d., https://erau.edu/partnerships#:~:text=Embry%2DRiddle%20partners%20with%20the,FAA)%2C%20and%20Diamond%20Aircraft (June 14, 2023).

12. Ellen Bara Stolzenberg, Melissa C. Aragon, Edgar Romo, Victoria Couch, Destiny McLennan, M. Kevin Eagan, and Nathaniel Kang, "The American Freshman: National Norms Fall 2019," *Higher Education Research Institute*, Monograph Series, 2020, https://www.heri.ucla.edu/monographs/TheAmericanFreshman2019.pdf (June 19, 2023).

13. Ray Schroeder, "Colleges Should Be Planning More Intentionally for Students Who Commute to Campuses This Fall," *Inside Higher Ed*, July 23, 2020, https://www.insidehighered.com/views/2020/07/23/colleges-should-be-planning-more-intentionally-students-who-commute-campuses-fall (June 21, 2023).

14. "Transfer Requirements," *University of California Admissions*, n.d., https://admission.universityofcalifornia.edu/admission-requirements/transfer-requirements (June 20, 2023).

15. "UC Berkeley Quick Facts," *Office of Planning and Analysis, UC Berkeley*, n.d., https://opa.berkeley.edu/campus-data/uc-berkeley-quick-facts (June 14, 2023).

16. "Harvard Undergraduates Are Teaching Each Other and Harvard Doesn't Want to Talk about It," *Harvard Political Review*, December 9, 2013, https://harvardpolitics.com/harvard-undergraduates-teaching-harvard-doesnt-want-talk/#:~:text=The%20Statistics%20department%20hired%2032,remain%20mute%20on%20the%20subject (June 21, 2023).

17. Karen W. Arenson, "Lining Up to Get a Lecture: A Class with 1,600 Students and One Popular Teacher," *New York Times*, November 17, 2000,

https://www.nytimes.com/2000/11/17/nyregion/lining-up-to-get-a-lecture-a
-class-with-1600-students-and-one-popular-teacher.html (June 21, 2023).

18. "Tuition Rates and Fees," *Cornell University Division of Financial Affairs*, n.d., https://www.dfa.cornell.edu/bursar/students-parents/tuition-rates -fees (June 14, 2023).

19. John T. McGreevy, "The Great Disappearing Teaching Load," *Chronicle of Higher Education*, February 3, 2019, https://www.chronicle.com/article /the-great-disappearing-teaching-load/?resetPassword=true&email=anna%40e ducation-rethink.com&success=true&bc_nonce=v91l22hry8bgtij4z01g6&cid =gen_sign_in (June 21, 2023).

20. Duke Cheston, "What a Load!," *James G. Martin Center for Academic Renewal*, January 7, 2011, https://www.jamesgmartin.center/2011/01/what-a -load (June 21, 2023).

21. Lynn O'Shaughnessy, "Why Don't Professors Like to Teach?," *CBS News*, December 20, 2010, https://www.cbsnews.com/news/why-dont-profes sors-like-to-teach (June 23, 2023).

22. Scott White, "Benefits of Attending a Less Selective College," *College Solution*, n.d., https://thecollegesolution.com/benefits-of-attending-a-less-select ive-college (June 21, 2023).

23. Tara A. Rose and Terri L. Flateby, "From College to Career Success," *Inside Higher Ed*, July 14, 2022, https://www.insidehighered.com/views /2022/07/15/employers-recent-grads-rate-their-skills-opinion (June 24, 2023).

24. "The Best Undergraduate Teaching National Universities," *U.S. News & World Report*, n.d., https://www.usnews.com/best-colleges/rankings/national -universities/undergraduate-teaching (June 25, 2023).

25. Anthony P. Carnevale, Ban Cheah, Martin Van Der Werf, and Artem Gulish, "Buyer Beware: First-Year Earnings and Debt for 37,000 College Majors at 4,400 Institutions," *CEW Georgetown*, November 19, 2020, https:// cew.georgetown.edu/cew-reports/collegemajorroi (June 24, 2023).

26. "Measuring the Most Important Outcomes of Higher Education," *Gallup-Purdue Index, Purdue Marketing and Media*, n.d., https://www.purdue .edu/newsroom/gallup (June 25, 2023).

27. Brianna McGurran, "College Tuition Inflation: A Historical Perspective," *Forbes*, May 9, 2023, https://www.forbes.com/advisor/student-loans /college-tuition-inflation (June 21, 2023).

28. "Employment Earnings," *Association of Public and Land-Grant Universities*, n.d., https://www.aplu.org/our-work/4-policy-and-advocacy/publicuvalues/employment-earnings (June 21, 2023).

29. "The Economic Value of College Majors," *Georgetown University Center on Education and the Workforce*, n.d., https://cew.georgetown.edu/cew-reports/valueofcollegemajors (June 21, 2023).

CHAPTER 8

1. "Admissions Statistics," *University of Oxford*, n.d., https://www.ox.ac.uk/about/facts-and-figures/admissions-statistics (June 19, 2023).

2. Douglas Broom, "These Are the Most Expensive Cities in the World," *World Economic Forum*, December 22, 2022, https://www.weforum.org/agenda/2022/12/world-most-expensive-cities (June 19, 2023).

3. Alexander Lobrano, "Meet the Two New French Cheeses Invented during Lockdown," *Food & Wine*, June 3, 2021, https://www.foodandwine.com/appetizers/antipasto/cheese/meet-the-two-new-french-cheeses-invented-during-lockdown (June 19, 2023).

4. Heather Wood Rudulph, "Get That Life: How I Became a Professional Pastry Chef," *Cosmopolitan*, November 1, 2021, https://www.cosmopolitan.com/career/a59847/caroline-schiff-greene-grape-get-that-life (June 19, 2023).

5. Anna Esaki-Smith, "How A Free Online Harvard Course Led a Bangalore Student to Help Walmart Develop Its Vaccine Portal," *Forbes*, May 18, 2021, https://www.forbes.com/sites/annaesakismith/2021/05/18/how-a-free-online-harvard-course-led-a-bangalore-student-to-help-walmart-develop-its-vaccine-portal/?sh=65b3bb37e3d2 (June 19, 2023).

6. "Academic Standing and Student Conduct Requirements for Degree Programs," *Harvard University Extension School*, n.d., https://extension.harvard.edu/registration-admissions/for-students/student-policies-conduct/academic-standing-and-student-conduct-requirements-for-degree-programs (June 20, 2023).

CHAPTER 9

1. Ivan Misner, "Networking Is More about Farming Than It Is about Hunting," *Dr. Ivan Misner®*, July 30, 2020, https://ivanmisner.com/networking-is-more-about-farming-than-it-is-about-hunting (June 14, 2023).

2. Garrett Lord, "Expanding Our Efforts to Help All Students Find Opportunity," *Handshake*, October 8, 2019, https://joinhandshake.com/blog/our-team/expanding-our-efforts-to-help-all-students-find-opportunity (June 14, 2023).

3. "See Where Michigan Technological University Ranks among the World's Best Universities," *U.S. News & World Report*, n.d., https://www.usnews.com/education/best-global-universities/michigan-technological-university-171128 (June 14, 2023).

4. "Michigan Technological University Overall Rankings | US News Best Colleges," *U.S. News & World Report*, n.d., https://www.usnews.com/best-colleges/michigan-tech-2292/overall-rankings#:~:text=Michigan%20Technological%20University%20is%20ranked,about%20how%20we%20rank%20schools (June 14, 2023).

5. Diya Khanna, "Why Mentorship and Sponsorship Are Critical to Women's Success," *UW Professional & Continuing Education*, May 25, 2022, https://www.pce.uw.edu/news-features/articles/mentorship-sponsorship-critical-womens-success (June 14, 2023).

6. "Adam Grant Ph.D.," *Psychology Today*, n.d., https://www.psychologytoday.com/us/contributors/adam-grant-phd (June 14, 2023).

CHAPTER 10

1. "A 4-Year Degree Isn't Quite the Job Requirement It Used to Be," *New York Times*, April 8, 2022, https://www.nytimes.com/2022/04/08/business/hiring-without-college-degree.html (June 19, 2023).

2. Ally Mintzer, "Paying Attention: The Attention Economy," *Berkeley Economic Review*, March 31, 2020, https://econreview.berkeley.edu/paying-attention-the-attention-economy (June 19, 2023).

3. "Cost of College Tuition Has Remained Stable since September 2019," *U.S. Bureau of Labor Statistics*, August 31, 2021, https://www.bls.gov/opub

/ted/2021/cost-of-college-tuition-has-remained-stable-since-september-2019.htm (June 19, 2023).

4. "Apple, IBM, and Google No Longer Require College Degrees for Employees," *The Made in America Movement*, May 8, 2019, https://www.the madeinamericamovement.com/news/apple-ibm-and-google-no-longer-require -college-degrees-for-employees (June 19, 2023).

5. Mearian Lucas, "Companies Move to Drop College Degree Requirements for New Hires, Focus on Skills," *Computerworld*, August 10, 2022, https:// www.computerworld.com/article/3669412/companies-move-to-drop-college -degree-requirements-for-new-hires-focus-on-skills.html (June 19, 2023).

6. "Grow with Google," *Grow with Google*, n.d., https://grow.google/cer tificates/?utm_source=google&utm_medium=paidsearch&utm_cam paign=ha-sem-bk-gen-phr__geo--US&utm_term=google%20certificate&gad =1&gclid=Cj0KCQjw98ujBhCgARIsAD7QeAhDtpHbCdAU08pNaQe _u1QfiSXw0x01XREKEsBBA_ePK2y7Zpblx0caAtICEALw_wcB#?modal _active=none (June 15, 2023).

7. "Apprenticeships," *Accenture*, n.d., https://www.accenture.com/us-en /about/company/apprenticeships (June 21, 2023).

8. "Apprenticeship Statistics 2021," *U.S. Department of Labor*, n.d., https:// www.dol.gov/agencies/eta/apprenticeship/about/statistics/2021#:~:text=In%20 FY%202021%2C%20more%20than,apprenticeship%20system%20in%20 FY%202021 (June 21, 2023).

9. Alex Keown, "Merck's Ken Frazier Named CEO of the Year," *BioSpace*, May 19, 2021, https://www.biospace.com/article/merck-s-ken-frazier-named -ceo-of-the-year (June 21, 2023).

10. Ginni Rometty, "6 Lessons I Learned Building a Culture That Recruits for 'Skills First' Not Just Degrees," *LinkedIn*, n.d., https://www.linkedin.com /pulse/6-lessons-i-learned-building-culture-recruits-skills-first-rometty (June 15, 2023).

11. "Reuters Launches the Reuters Digital Journalism Course in Partnership with the Facebook Journalism Project," https://www.reutersagency.com/pt-br /media-center/reuters-launches-the-reuters-digital-journalism-course-in-part nership-with-the-facebook-journalism-project (June 15, 2023).

12. "Cost of Attendance," *Columbia University Graduate School of Journalism*, n.d., https://journalism.columbia.edu/cost-attendance (June 28, 2023).

13. "Employment and Wage Estimates for Newspaper Journalists," *U.S. Bureau of Labor Statistics*, n.d., https://www.bls.gov/oes/current/oes273023.htm (June 28, 2023).

14. "Construction Workforce Shortage Tops Half a Million in 2023, Says ABC | News Releases," *ABC*, n.d., February 9, 2023, https://www.abc.org/News-Media/News-Releases/entryid/19777/construction-workforce-shortage-tops-half-a-million-in-2023-says-abc (June 15, 2023).

15. Trey Howard, "New Technology Contributing to Nationwide Auto Technician Shortage," *WDAM7*, February 25, 2023, https://www.wdam.com/2023/02/25/new-technology-contributing-nationwide-auto-technician-shortage (June 21, 2023).

16. Kate Magill, "With More Than 800K Unfilled Jobs, Manufacturers Strain to Attract Talent," *Manufacturing Dive*, November 14, 2022, https://www.manufacturingdive.com/news/manufacturing-labor-workforce-shortages-2023-outlook-deloitte-national-association-manufacturers/636275 (June 21, 2023).

17. Amy Chan, "Carpenters in High Demand According to U.S. Builders," *Contractor News*, June 10, 2022, https://www.contractornews.com/498/carpenters-in-high-demand-according-to-u.s.-builders (June 15, 2023).

18. Grace Mayer, "More Students Are Learning to Be Mechanics, Chefs, and Construction Workers as College Enrollment Shrinks," *Business Insider*, April 20, 2023, https://www.businessinsider.com/culinary-mechanics-construction-trade-program-increase-college-enrollment-decreases-study-2023-4 (June 21, 2023).

19. Olivia Sanchez, "Why Many Students Are Choosing Trade Programs over College," *Christian Science Monitor*, April 21, 2023, https://www.csmonitor.com/USA/Education/2023/0417/Why-many-students-are-choosing-trade-programs-over-college (June 21, 2023).

20. Jon Marcus, "High-Paying Jobs That Don't Need a College Degree? Thousands of Them Sit Empty," *NPR*, February 14, 2023, https://www.npr.org/2023/02/14/1155405249/high-paying-jobs-that-dont-need-a-college-degree-thousands-of-them-are-sitting-e (June 21, 2023).

21. "About Us | The Good Jobs Project," *The Good Jobs Project*, September 9, 2019, https://goodjobsdata.org/about-cew/#:~:text=The%20Good%20Jobs%20Project%2C%20a%20research%20project%20by,workers%20who%20do%20not%20have%20a%20bachelor%E2%80%99s%20degree (June 21, 2023).

CHAPTER 11

1. Abigail Johnson Hess, "74% of Colleges Face Financial Challenges, according to Survey of Higher-Ed Workers," *CNBC*, August 25, 2021, https://www.cnbc.com/2021/08/25/74percent-of-colleges-face-financial-challenges-according-to-survey-of-higher-ed-workers.html (June 19, 2023).

2. "Undergraduate Enrollment," *National Center for Education Statistics*, May 2023, https://nces.ed.gov/programs/coe/indicator/cha/undergrad-enrollment#:~:text=Between%20fall%202010%20and%20fall,percent%20to%2016.8%20million%20students (June 28, 2023).

3. John Fink, "What Happened to Community College Enrollment during the First Years of the Pandemic? It Depends on the Students' Age," *Community College Research Center, Teachers College, Columbia University*, January 9, 2023, https://ccrc.tc.columbia.edu/easyblog/what-happened-to-community-college-enrollment-depends-students-age.html (June 29, 2023).

4. "Public School Enrollment," *National Center for Education Statistics*, May 2023, https://nces.ed.gov/programs/coe/indicator/cga/public-school-enrollment (June 19, 2023).

5. "Home | Scholarship Momma," *Scholarship Momma*, n.d., https://www.scholarshipmomma.com/#:~:text=Federal%20Reserve%20Average%20Student%20Loan%20Debt%20%241.75%20trillion,students%20from%20public%20four-year%20institutions%20had%20student%20loans (June 15, 2023).

6. "Tuition Discount Rates at Private Colleges and Universities Hit All-Time Highs," *Nacubo*, May 19, 2022, https://www.nacubo.org/Press-Releases/2022/Tuition%20Discount%20Rates%20at%20Private%20Colleges%20and%20Universities%20Hit%20All%20Time%20Highs#:~:text=In%20AY%202021-22%2C%2082.5%20percent%20of%20all%20undergraduates,of%2060.7%20percent%20of%20published%20tuition%20and%20fees (June 15, 2023).

7. James Paterson, "Moody's: Slow Enrollment Gains Raise Colleges' Financial Risk," *Higher Ed Dive*, March 7, 2019, https://www.highereddive.com/news/moodys-slow-enrollment-gains-raise-colleges-financial-risk/549960 (June 21, 2023).

8. Anemona Hartocollis, "A Sign That Tuition Is Too High: Some Colleges Are Slashing It in Half," *New York Times*, December 14, 2022, https://www.nytimes.com/2022/12/14/us/college-universities-college-tuition-reset.html#:~:text=Nearly%20a%20third%20of%20parents%20and%20students

%20believe,at%20some%20point%20because%20of%20its%20high%20cost (June 21, 2023).

9. Hartocollis, "A Sign That Tuition Is Too High."

10. "Colby-Sawyer College Expands Opportunities with New $17,500 Tuition," *Colby-Sawyer College*, September 7, 2022, https://colby-sawyer .edu/news/colby-sawyer-college-expands-opportunities-with-new-17-500 -tuition#:~:text=After%20years%20of%20strategic%20planning%20and%20 decisive%20action,Colby-Sawyer%20is%20reducing%20its%20tuition%20 by%2062%20percent (June 14, 2023).

11. Kris Stokes, "Closing the Skills Gap 2023," *Wiley*, January 24, 2023, https://universityservices.wiley.com/closing-the-skills-gap-2023 (June 21, 2023).

12. Andrew Van Dam, "The Most-Regretted (and Lowest-Paying) College Majors," *Washington Post*, September 2, 2022, https://www.washingtonpost .com/business/2022/09/02/college-major-regrets (June 21, 2023).

13. "Survey of Household Economics and Decisionmaking," *Federal Reserve*, n.d., https://www.federalreserve.gov/consumerscommunities/shed.htm (June 15, 2023).

CHAPTER 12

1. Kimberlee Speakman, "New Orleans High School Student Receives Record $9M in Scholarship Offers from 125 Colleges," *People*, April 25, 2023, https://people.com/human-interest/new-orleans-high-school-student-receives -record-9m-in-scholarship-offers-from-125-colleges (June 22, 2023).

2. "How Shopify Went from Selling Snowboards to an E-Commerce Giant, Explained," *LinkedIn*, February 9, 2022, https://www.linkedin.com/pulse /how-shopify-went-from-selling-snowboards-ecommerce-giant-explained- (July 3, 2023).

3. Stuart Dredge, "YouTube Was Meant to Be a Video-Dating Website," *The Guardian*, March 16, 2016, https://www.theguardian.com/technology/2016 mar/16/youtube-past-video-dating-website (July 3, 2023).

4. Megan Garber, "Instagram Was First Called Burbn," *The Atlantic*, July 2, 2014, https://www.theatlantic.com/technology/archive/2014/07/instagram-used-to-be-called-brbn/373815 (July 3, 2023).

5. Tara Bitran, "Netflix Trivia: Celebrating 25 Years of Entertainment," *Netflix*, August 29, 2022, https://www.netflix.com/tudum/articles/netflix-trivia-25th-anniversary (July 3, 2023).

BIBLIOGRAPHY

Abel, Jason R., and Richard Deitz. "Despite Rising Costs, College Is Still a Good Investment." *Liberty Street Economics*. June 16, 2021. https://liberty streeteconomics.newyorkfed.org/2019/06/despite-rising-costs-college-is -still-a-good-investment (June 5, 2023).

"About Us." *The Good Jobs Project*. September 9, 2019. https://goodjobsdata .org/about-cew/#:~:text=The%20Good%20Jobs%20Project%2C%20a%20 research%20project%20by,workers%20who%20do%20not%20have%20 a%20bachelor%E2%80%99s%20degree (June 21, 2023).

"A Brief History of New York University." *New York University Web Communications*. n.d. https://www.nyu.edu/faculty/governance-policies-and-pro cedures/faculty-handbook/the-university/history-and-traditions-of-new-york -university/a-brief-history-of-new-york-university.html (June 13, 2023).

"Academic Credit and Class Levels." *UCLA Catalog*. n.d. https://catalog.regis trar.ucla.edu/Policies-and-Regulations/Academic-Policies/Academic-Credit -and-Class-Levels (June 3, 2023).

"Academic Standing and Student Conduct Requirements for Degree Programs." *Harvard University Extension School*. n.d. https://extension.harvard .edu/registration-admissions/for-students/student-policies-conduct/aca demic-standing-and-student-conduct-requirements-for-degree-programs (June 20, 2023).

"Adam Grant Ph.D." *Psychology Today*. n.d. https://www.psychologytoday
.com/us/contributors/adam-grant-phd (June 14, 2023).

"Admissions Statistics." *University of Oxford*. n.d. https://www.ox.ac.uk/about
/facts-and-figures/admissions-statistics (June 19, 2023).

"A 4-Year Degree Isn't Quite the Job Requirement It Used to Be." *New York
Times*. April 8, 2022. https://www.nytimes.com/2022/04/08/business/hiring
-without-college-degree.html (June 19, 2023).

"All Tony Awards Won by Carnegie Mellon University Faculty, Students
and Alumni." *Carnegie Mellon University*. n.d. https://www.cmu.edu/about
/awards.html#AllTonyAwards (June 13, 2023).

Alter, Alexandra, and Elizabeth A. Harris. "What Snoop Dogg's Success Says
about the Book Industry." *New York Times*. April 28, 2021. https://www.ny
times.com/2021/04/18/books/book-sales-publishing-pandemic-coronavirus
.html (June 11, 2023).

Amponsah, Michelle N., and Emma H. Haidar. "Harvard College Accepts
3.41% of Applicants to Class of 2027." *Harvard Crimson*. March 31, 2023.
https://www.thecrimson.com/article/2023/3/31/admissions-decisions-2027
(June 2, 2023).

Anders, George. "Who's Vaulting into the C-Suite? Trends Changed Fast in
2022." *LinkedIn*. February 1, 2023. https://www.linkedin.com/pulse/whos
-vaulting-c-suite-trends-changed-fast-2022-george-anders (June 15, 2023).

"Apple, IBM, and Google No Longer Require College Degrees for Employees."
The Made in America Movement. May 8, 2019. https://www.themadeinamerica
movement.com/news/apple-ibm-and-google-no-longer-require-college
-degrees-for-employees (June 19, 2023).

"Apprenticeships." *Accenture*. n.d. https://www.accenture.com/us-en/about
/company/apprenticeships (June 21, 2023).

"Apprenticeships." *Unilever.com*. n.d. https://careers.unilever.com/uk-appren
ticeships (June 20, 2023).

"Apprenticeship Statistics 2021." *U.S. Department of Labor*. n.d. https://www
.dol.gov/agencies/eta/apprenticeship/about/statistics/2021#:~:text=In%20
FY%202021%2C%20more%20than,apprenticeship%20system%20in%20
FY%202021 (June 21, 2023).

Arenson, Karen W. "Lining Up to Get a Lecture: A Class with 1,600 Students
and One Popular Teacher." *New York Times*. November 17, 2000. https://

www.nytimes.com/2000/11/17/nyregion/lining-up-to-get-a-lecture-a-class
-with-1600-students-and-one-popular-teacher.html (June 21, 2023).

"Ariana Grande Quotes." Goodreads. n.d. https://www.goodreads.com/quotes
/search?q=Ariana+grande (June 13, 2023).

"Average Vogue Salary: By Location, Job Title, and Department." Zippia.
August 22, 2022. https://www.zippia.com/vogue-careers-68033/salary (June
15, 2023).

Bahney, Anna. "Manhattan Median Rents Hit Another High in March." *CNN
Business*. April 13, 2023. https://edition.cnn.com/2023/04/13/homes/man
hattan-rentals-march/index.html (June 13, 2023).

Bailey, Angela. "CHCO Blog—Light the Fire within You." *Department
of Homeland Security*. February 3, 2021. https://www.dhs.gov/employee
-resources/blog/2021/02/03/chco-blog-light-fire-within-you (June 13, 2023).

"Barack Obama's Feb. 5 Speech." *New York Times*. February 6, 2008.
https://www.nytimes.com/2008/02/05/us/politics/05text-obama.html (June
6, 2023).

Barshay, Jill. "PROOF POINTS: The Number of College Graduates in the
Humanities Drops for the Eighth Consecutive Year." *The Hechinger Report*.
November 23, 2021. https://hechingerreport.org/proof-points-the-number
-of-college-graduates-in-the-humanities-drops-for-the-eighth-consecutive
-year (June 14, 2023).

Belkin, Douglas. "For Sale: SAT Takers' Names. Colleges Buy Student Data
and Boost Exclusivity." *Wall Street Journal*. November 5, 2019. https://
www.wsj.com/articles/for-sale-sat-takers-names-colleges-buy-student-data
-and-boost-exclusivity-11572976621 (June 13, 2023).

Betts, Anna, Andrew Little, Elizabeth Sander, Alexandra Tremayne-Pengelly,
and Walt Bogdanich. "How Colleges and Sports-Betting Companies 'Cae-
sarized' Campuses." *New York Times*. November 20, 2022. https://www.ny
times.com/2022/11/20/business/caesars-sports-betting-universities-colleges
.html (June 1, 2023).

Binaykia, Arnav. "NYU Acceptance Rate Drops to 8% for Class of 2027." *Washington Square News*. March 28, 2023. https://nyunews.com/news/2023/03/29
/nyu-admission-rate-class-of-2027 (June 14, 2023).

Bitran, Tara. "Netflix Trivia: Celebrating 25 Years of Entertainment." *Netflix*.
August 29, 2022. https://www.netflix.com/tudum/articles/netflix-trivia-25th
-anniversary (July 3, 2023).

Brahm, Nikki. "Experts Call for Increased Asian American Studies to Counter Ignorance and Hate." *INSIGHT Into Diversity.* May 20, 2023. https://www.insightintodiversity.com/experts-call-for-increased-asian-american-studies-to-counter-ignorance-and-hate (June 16, 2023).

Broom, Douglas. "These Are the Most Expensive Cities in the World." *World Economic Forum.* December 22, 2022. https://www.weforum.org/agenda/2022/12/world-most-expensive-cities (June 19, 2023).

Brown, Mike. "Which U.S. Colleges Make the Most Revenue from Applications?" *LendEDU.* April 6, 2023. https://lendedu.com/blog/which-colleges-make-most-revenue-from-applications (June 13, 2023).

Bui, Quoctrung. "How 'Build Your Own College Rankings' Was Built." *New York Times.* March 27, 2023. https://www.nytimes.com/2023/03/27/opinion/how-build-your-own-college-rankings-was-built.html (June 13, 2023).

"Can Artificial Intelligence Perfect Mammography?" *NYU Langone Health.* n.d. https://nyulangone.org/news/can-artificial-intelligence-perfect-mammography (June 2, 2023).

CareerBuilder Hiring Solutions. "The Skills Gap Is Costing Companies Nearly $1 Million Annually, According to New CareerBuilder Survey." *Press Room, Career Builder.* April 13, 2017. https://press.careerbuilder.com/2017-04-13-The-Skills-Gap-is-Costing-Companies-Nearly-1-Million-Annually-According-to-New-CareerBuilder-Survey#:~:text=According%20to%20a%20new%20CareerBuilder,is%20more%20than%20%24800%2C000%20annually (June 15, 2023).

"Carnegie Mellon to Become First Exclusive Higher Education Partner of the Tony Awards." *Tony Awards.* n.d. https://www.tonyawards.com/press/carnegie-mellon-to-become-first-exclusive-higher-education-partner-of-the-tony-awards (June 13, 2023).

Carnevale, Anthony P., Ban Cheah, Martin Van Der Werf, and Artem Gulish. "Buyer Beware: First-Year Earnings and Debt for 37,000 College Majors at 4,400 Institutions." *CEW Georgetown.* November 19, 2020. https://cew.georgetown.edu/cew-reports/collegemajorroi (June 24, 2023).

Carter, Jamie. "Jeff Bezos' Blue Origin Bags New NASA Contract for Mars Mission." *Forbes.* February 10, 2023. https://www.forbes.com/sites/jamiecartereurope/2023/02/10/jeff-bezos-blue-origin-bags-new-nasa-contract-for-mars-mission/?sh=51fc93fd2015 (June 14, 2023).

Carter, Shawn M. "Colleges Make a Fortune from Saying 'No' to Applications—Here's How Much." *CNBC*. September 28, 2017. https://www.cnbc.com/2017/09/28/how-much-money-colleges-make-rejecting-students-applications.html (June 13, 2023).

Chadha, Dhriti. "NYU Acceptance Rate | What Are Your Chances of Getting In?" *Study Abroad Blogs | All About Universities, Programs, Tests, & More!* February 12, 2023. https://ischoolconnect.com/blog/nyu-acceptance-rate-what-are-your-chances-of-getting-in (June 13, 2023).

Chan, Amy. "Carpenters in High Demand According to U.S. Builders." *Contractor News*. June 10, 2022. https://www.contractornews.com/498/carpenters-in-high-demand-according-to-u.s.-builders (June 15, 2023).

Chen, Lulu Yilun. "Alibaba." *Bloomberg.com*. November 20, 2017. https://www.bloomberg.com/quicktake/alibaba#xj4y7vzkg (June 9, 2023).

Cheston, Duke. "What a Load!" *James G. Martin Center for Academic Renewal*. January 7, 2011. https://www.jamesgmartin.center/2011/01/what-a-load (June 21, 2023).

"Chicago Housing Market." *Redfin*. n.d. https://www.redfin.com/city/29470/IL/Chicago/housing-market (June 14, 2023).

Clark, Simon, and Margot Patrick. "HSBC Appoints Noel Quinn as Permanent CEO." *Wall Street Journal*. March 17, 2020. https://www.wsj.com/articles/hsbc-appoints-noel-quinn-as-permanent-ceo-11584469873 (June 13, 2023).

Clifford, Catherine. "Billionaire Mark Cuban: 'One of the Great Lies of Life Is Follow Your Passions.'" *CNBC*. November 13, 2020. https://www.cnbc.com/2018/02/16/mark-cuban-follow-your-passion-is-bad-advice.html#:~:text=%E2%80%9COne%20of%20the%20great%20lies%20of%20life%20is%20'follow%20your,what%20you%20are%20passionate%20about (June 14, 2023).

———. "Jeff Bezos Says This Is How He Plans to Spend the Bulk of His Fortune." *CNBC*. April 30, 2018. https://www.cnbc.com/2018/04/30/jeff-bezos-says-this-is-how-he-plans-to-spend-the-bulk-of-his-fortune.html#:~:text=Bezos%20says%20his%20work%20on%20Blue%20Origin%2C%20his,continue%20to%20do%20that%20for%20a%20long%20time (June 14, 2023).

———. "Jeff Bezos: You Can't Pick Your Passions." *CNBC*. February 7, 2019. https://www.cnbc.com/2019/02/07/amazon-and-blue-origins-jeff-bezos-on-identifying-your-passion.html (June 13, 2023).

Clips, Lex. "Steve Jobs: The Only Way to Do Great Work Is to Love What You Do." December 25, 2019. https://www.youtube.com/watch?v=JV 3OqaRmBk4 (June 14, 2023).

Colby-Sawyer College. "Colby-Sawyer College Expands Opportunities with New $17,500 Tuition." September 7, 2022. https://colby-sawyer.edu /news/colby-sawyer-college-expands-opportunities-with-new-17-500 -tuition#:~:text=After%20years%20of%20strategic%20planning%20and%20 decisive%20action,Colby-Sawyer%20is%20reducing%20its%20tuition%20 by%2062%20percent (June 14, 2023).

"Colleges with Great Writing Programs." *U.S. News & World Report*. n.d. https://www.usnews.com/best-colleges/rankings/writing-programs (June 2, 2023).

"Combination of Artificial Intelligence and Radiologists More Accurately Identified Breast Cancer." *NYU Langone Health*. October 17, 2019. https:// nyulangone.org/news/combination-artificial-intelligence-radiologists-more -accurately-identified-breast-cancer (June 13, 2023).

"Construction Workforce Shortage Tops Half a Million in 2023, Says ABC | News Releases." *ABC*. n.d. https://www.abc.org/News-Media/News-Releases /entryid/19777/construction-workforce-shortage-tops-half-a-million-in -2023-says-abc (June 15, 2023).

"Cost & Affordability." *Columbia Undergraduate Admissions*. n.d. https:// undergrad.admissions.columbia.edu/affordability/cost (June 20, 2023).

"Cost of Attendance." *Columbia University Graduate School of Journalism*. n.d. https://journalism.columbia.edu/cost-attendance (June 28, 2023).

"Cost of Attendance." *Harvey Mudd College*. n.d. https://www.hmc.edu/admis sion/afford/cost-of-attendance (June 19, 2023).

"Cost of College Tuition Has Remained Stable since September 2019." *U.S. Bureau of Labor Statistics*. August 31, 2021. https://www.bls.gov/opub /ted/2021/cost-of-college-tuition-has-remained-stable-since-september-2019 .htm (June 19, 2023).

"Cost to Attend | Financial Aid." *Cornell University*. n.d. https://finaid.cornell .edu/cost-attend (June 15, 2023).

"Creating Your Own Job Opportunities." *UW Professional & Continuing Education*. February 1, 2015. https://www.pce.uw.edu/news-features/articles /creating-your-own-job-opportunities (June 3, 2023).

"CSU San Marcos Tops Ninth Annual Social Mobility Index of Schools Driving the American Dream through Their Ethos and Action." *Business wire.com*. November 4, 2022. https://www.businesswire.com/news/home /20221104005031/en (June 14, 2023).

Curran, David. "UC Acceptance Rates 1997–2017." *SFGATE*. March 29, 2018. https://www.sfgate.com/news/slideshow/UC-acceptance-rates -1997-2017-179965.php (June 3, 2023).

"Current Term Enrollment Estimates." *National Student Clearinghouse Research Center*. May 24, 2023. https://nscresearchcenter.org/current-term -enrollment-estimates (June 10, 2023).

Custer, C. "Tech in Asia—Connecting Asia's Startup Ecosystem." *Tech in Asia*. May 14, 2015. https://www.techinasia.com/jack-ma-what-told-son-education (June 8, 2023).

CyberSeek. "Cybersecurity Remains One of the Most in Demand Professions, New Data from CyberSeek Confirms." *PR Newswire*. October 17, 2022. https://www.prnewswire.com/news-releases/cybersecurity-remains -one-of-the-most-in-demand-professions-new-data-from-cyberseek-con firms-301651014.html (June 10, 2023).

D'Amato, Pete. "University of Chicago Projected to Be the First U.S. University to Charge $100,000 a Year." *Hechinger Report*. October 30, 2019. https:// hechingerreport.org/university-of-chicago-projected-to-be-the-first-u-s-uni versity-to-charge-100000-a-year (June 20, 2023).

Dickler, Jessica. "Scrub Daddy CEO Credits College for His Clean Start." *CNBC*. June 26, 2017. https://www.cnbc.com/2017/06/23/scrub-daddy-ceo -credits-college-for-his-start-in-the-sponge-business.html (June 14, 2023).

Dodds, Klaus. "Skiing in the Alps Faces a Bleak Future Thanks to Climate Change." *PhysOrg.com*. December 31, 2022. https://phys.org/news/2022 -12-alps-bleak-future-climate.html (June 5, 2023).

Dolan, Kerry A. "Forbes' 35th Annual World's Billionaires List: Facts and Figures 2021." *Forbes*. April 6, 2021. https://www.forbes.com/sites/kerrya dolan/2021/04/06/forbes-35th-annual-worlds-billionaires-list-facts-and-figu res-2021/?sh=61a4ca885e58 (June 13, 2023).

Dredge, Stuart. "YouTube Was Meant to Be a Video-Dating Website." *The Guardian*. March 16, 2016. https://www.theguardian.com/technology/2016 /mar/16/youtube-past-video-dating-website (July 3, 2023).

"Employment and Wage Estimates for Newspaper Journalists." *U.S. Bureau of Labor Statistics.* n.d. https://www.bls.gov/oes/current/oes273023.htm (June 28, 2023).

"Employment Earnings." *Association of Public and Land-Grant Universities.* n.d. https://www.aplu.org/our-work/4-policy-and-advocacy/publicuvalues /employment-earnings (June 21, 2023).

Esaki-Smith, Anna. "How A Free Online Harvard Course Led a Bangalore Student to Help Walmart Develop Its Vaccine Portal." *Forbes.* May 18, 2021. https://www.forbes.com/sites/annaesakismith/2021/05/18/how-a-free -online-harvard-course-led-a-bangalore-student-to-help-walmart-develop-its -vaccine-portal/?sh=65b3bb37e3d2 (June 19, 2023).

———. "US Renews Commitment to International Students and Presence on 'World Stage.'" *Forbes.* July 27, 2021. https://www.forbes.com /sites/annaesakismith/2021/07/26/us-renews-commitment-to-international -students-and-presence-on-world-stage/?sh=451382704236 (June 13, 2023).

———. "Yale Law School Withdraws from U.S. News Rankings over Methodology." *Forbes.* November 16, 2022. https://www.forbes.com/sites/annaesaki smith/2022/11/16/yale-law-school-withdraws-from-us-news-rankings-over -methodology/?sh=7fb48d0726c7 (June 13, 2023).

"Executive Summary | Teens and Tech 2022." *Institute for Family Studies.* n.d. https://ifstudies.org/reports/teens-and-tech/2022/executive-summary (June 5, 2023).

"Fast Facts: Enrollment (98)." National Center for Education Statistics. n.d. https://nces.ed.gov/fastfacts/display.asp?id=98 (June 15, 2023).

Fink, John. "What Happened to Community College Enrollment during the First Years of the Pandemic? It Depends on the Students' Age." *Community College Research Center, Teachers College, Columbia University.* January 9, 2023. https://ccrc.tc.columbia.edu/easyblog/what-happened-to-community -college-enrollment-depends-students-age.html (June 29, 2023).

"Freshman Admit Data | UC Admissions." *University of California.* n.d. https:// admission.universityofcalifornia.edu/campuses-majors/berkeley/freshman -admit-data.html (June 6, 2023).

Fry, Richard. "Millennials Outnumbered Boomers in 2019." *Pew Research Center.* May 22, 2023. https://www.pewresearch.org/fact-tank/2020/04/28 /millennials-overtake-baby-boomers-as-americas-largest-generation (June 6, 2023).

Garber, Megan. "Instagram Was First Called Burbn." *The Atlantic*. July 2, 2014. https://www.theatlantic.com/technology/archive/2014/07/instagram-used-to-be-called-brbn/373815 (July 3, 2023).

Gill, John Freeman. "Restoring Brooklyn's Queen of Department Stores." *New York Times*. November 22, 2019. https://www.nytimes.com/2019/11/22/realestate/restoring-brooklyns-queen-of-department-stores.html (June 15, 2023).

Gilmore, Janet. "UC Berkeley Sees Record Number of Freshman Applications." *UC Berkeley News Archive*. April 5, 2007. https://newsarchive.berkeley.edu/news/media/releases/2007/04/05_admissions.shtml#:~:text=Although%20the%20number%20of%20individual,from%2023.6%20in%20fall%202006 (June 5, 2023).

Glasspiegel, Ryan. "Shohei Ohtani Gave Rousing World Baseball Classic Speech to Team Japan." *New York Post*. March 22, 2023. https://nypost.com/2023/03/21/shohei-ohtani-rallies-japan-with-pre-wbc-final-speech (July 2, 2023).

Goering, Laurie. "Solar-Power Internet Downloads Opportunities for African Refugees." *Reuters*. November 17, 2022. https://www.reuters.com/business/cop/solar-power-internet-downloads-opportunities-african-refugees-2022-11-17 (June 12, 2023).

Goldstein, Dana, and Stephanie Saul. "College Board Will Change Its AP African American Studies Course." *New York Times*. April 25, 2023. https://www.nytimes.com/2023/04/24/us/ap-african-american-studies-college-board.html (June 15, 2023).

"Google Entry Level Software Engineer Salaries." *Glassdoor*. n.d. https://www.glassdoor.com/Salary/Google-Entry-Level-Software-Engineer-Salaries-E9079_D_KO7,36.htm (June 10, 2022).

Gough, Neil, and Alexandra Stevenson. "The Unlikely Ascent of Jack Ma, Alibaba's Founder." *New York Times*. May 7, 2014. https://www.nytimes.com/2014/05/08/technology/the-unlikely-ascent-of-jack-ma-alibabas-founder.html (June 8, 2023).

"Great Barrier Reef Has Lost Half of Its Corals since 1995." *BBC News*. October 14, 2020. https://www.bbc.com/news/world-australia-54533971 (June 15, 2023).

Green, Alison. "Why Employers Don't Like Long-Distance Job Candidates." *U.S. News & World Report*. July 7, 2014. https://money.usnews.com/money

/blogs/outside-voices-careers/2014/07/07/why-employers-dont-like-long
-distance-job-candidates (June 16, 2023).

"Grow with Google." *Grow with Google*. n.d. https://grow.google/certificates
/?utm_source=google&utm_medium=paidsearch&utm_campaign=ha-sem
-bk-gen-phr__geo--US&utm_term=google%20certificate&gad=1&gcl
id=Cj0KCQjw98ujBhCgARIsAD7QeAhDtpHbCdAU08pNaQe_u1Q
fiSXw0x01XREKEsBBA_ePK2y7Zpblx0caAtICEALw_wcB#?modal
_active=none (June 15, 2023).

Hamilton, "Digital #Ham4Ham 1/17/16—'Martin Luther King,' Words &
Music by Barbara Ames." *YouTube*. January 17, 2016. https://www.youtube
.com/watch?v=7EITcerK6kM (June 13, 2023).

Hanson, Melanie. "Average Cost of College [2023]: Yearly Tuition + Expenses." *Education Data Initiative*. May 18, 2023. https://educationdata.org
/average-cost-of-college (June 20, 2023).

Hargett-Robinson, Adisa. "Florida Teen Accepted into 27 Universities with $4
Million in Scholarships." *Good Morning America*. April 13, 2022. https://
www.goodmorningamerica.com/living/story/florida-teen-accepted-27-uni
versities-million-scholarships-84030228 (June 3, 2023).

Hartocollis, Anemona. "A Sign That Tuition Is Too High: Some Colleges
Are Slashing It in Half." *New York Times*. December 14, 2022. https://www
.nytimes.com/2022/12/14/us/college-universities-college-tuition-reset.html
(June 21, 2023).

"Harvard Admits 3.4% of Students to the Class of 2027." *Crimson Education*.
March 31, 2023. https://www.crimsoneducation.org/us/blog/harvard-accept
ance-rate (June 14, 2023).

"Harvard Undergraduates Are Teaching Each Other and Harvard Doesn't Want
to Talk about It." *Harvard Political Review*. December 9, 2013. https://
harvardpolitics.com/harvard-undergraduates-teaching-harvard-doesnt-want
-talk/#:~:text=The%20Statistics%20department%20hired%2032,remain%20
mute%20on%20the%20subject (June 21, 2023).

Hecht, Evan. "What Years Are Gen X? A Detailed Breakdown of When Each
Generation Was Born." *USA Today*. May 9, 2023. https://www.usatoday
.com/story/news/2022/09/02/what-years-gen-x-millennials-baby-boomers
-gen-z/10303085002 (June 6, 2023).

Hess, Abigail Johnson. "74% of Colleges Face Financial Challenges, according
to Survey of Higher-Ed Workers." *CNBC*. August 25, 2021. https://www

.cnbc.com/2021/08/25/74percent-of-colleges-face-financial-challenges
-according-to-survey-of-higher-ed-workers.html (June 19, 2023).

"History Timeline." *HSBC Holdings Plc.* n.d. https://www.hsbc.com/who-we
-are/our-history/history-timeline (June 4, 2023).

"Home | Scholarship Momma." *Scholarship Momma.* n.d. https://www.scholar
shipmomma.com/#:~:text=Federal%20Reserve%20Average%20Student%20
Loan%20Debt%20%241.75%20trillion,students%20from%20public%20
four-year%20institutions%20had%20student%20loans (June 19, 2023).

"How Shopify Went from Selling Snowboards to an E-Commerce Giant, Explained." *LinkedIn.* February 9, 2022. https://www.linkedin.com/pulse/how
-shopify-went-from-selling-snowboards-ecommerce-giant-explained- (July 3,
2023).

Howard, Trey. "New Technology Contributing to Nationwide Auto Technician Shortage." *WDAM7.* February 25, 2023. https://www.wdam.com
/2023/02/25/new-technology-contributing-nationwide-auto-technician
-shortage (June 21, 2023).

"Jack Ma: Don't Try to Be the Best, Be the First!" *YouTube.* n.d. https://www
.youtube.com/watch?v=Uiztg_i0P9g (June 15, 2023).

Jacob, Mary K. "Manhattan Rents Reach All-Time High at $4,175 per
Month as Exodus Continues." *New York Post.* April 13, 2023. https://
nypost.com/2023/04/13/manhattan-median-rents-reach-an-all-time-high-of
-4175-month (June 15, 2023).

Jacobo, Julia. "Coral Reefs Could Stop Growing in 10 Years unless Greenhouse Gases Are Significantly Reduced, New Study Says." *ABC News.* May
11, 2021. https://abcnews.go.com/International/coral-reefs-stop-growing
-80-years-greenhouse-gases/story?id=77532016 (June 13, 2023).

Johnson, Holly. "Scrub Daddy: The Story behind Shark Tank US's Biggest
Success." *CEO Magazine.* February 8, 2019. https://www.theceomagazine
.com/business/innovation-technology/scrub-daddy-the-story-behind-shark
-tank-uss-biggest-success (June 15, 2023).

"Jon Hamm 'Might Still' Go Back to Teaching—and He Has a Name for the Class."
Today. January 20, 2023. https://www.today.com/video/jon-hamm-might
-still-go-back-to-teaching-and-he-has-a-name-for-the-class-957938755685
(June 13, 2023).

Keown, Alex. "Merck's Ken Frazier Named CEO of the Year." *BioSpace*. May 19, 2021. https://www.biospace.com/article/merck-s-ken-frazier-named-ceo -of-the-year (June 21, 2023).

Khanna, Diya. "Why Mentorship and Sponsorship Are Critical to Women's Success." *UW Professional & Continuing Education*. May 25, 2022. https:// www.pce.uw.edu/news-features/articles/mentorship-sponsorship-critical -womens-success (June 14, 2023).

Krutsch, Emily, and Victoria Roderick. "STEM Day: Explore Growing Careers." *U.S. Department of Labor Blog*. November 4, 2022. https://blog.dol.gov /2022/11/04/stem-day-explore-growing-careers#:~:text=In%20 2021%2C%20there%20were%20nearly%2010%20million%20 workers,STEM%20occupations%2C%20compared%20to%20%2 440%2C120%20for%20non-STEM%20occupations (June 13, 2023).

Lobrano, Alexander. "Meet the Two New French Cheeses Invented during Lockdown." *Food & Wine*. June 3, 2021. https://www.foodandwine.com/ap petizers/antipasto/cheese/meet-the-two-new-french-cheeses-invented-during -lockdown (June 19, 2023).

Lord, Garrett. "Expanding Our Efforts to Help All Students Find Opportunity." *Handshake*. October 8, 2019. https://joinhandshake.com/blog/our-team /expanding-our-efforts-to-help-all-students-find-opportunity (June 14, 2023).

Macmillan, Valerie, J. "Acceptance Rate Is Lowest of Ivies." *Harvard Crimson*. April 12, 1995. https://www.thecrimson.com/article/1995/4/12/acceptance -rate-is-lowest-of-ivies (June 3, 2023).

Magill, Kate. "With More Than 800K Unfilled Jobs, Manufacturers Strain to Attract Talent." *Manufacturing Dive*. November 14, 2022. https://www.manu facturingdive.com/news/manufacturing-labor-workforce-shortages-2023-out look-deloitte-national-association-manufacturers/636275 (June 21, 2023).

Mak, Robin. "Breakingviews—E-Commerce Can Be Open Sesame for Alibaba's Worth." *Reuters*. April 6, 2023. https://www.reuters.com/breakingviews /e-commerce-can-be-open-sesame-alibabas-worth-2023-04-06 (June 13, 2023).

Manning, Jeff. "Phil Knight's University of Oregon Donations Push $1 Billion Mark with New Hayward Field Project." *Oregonlive*. March 9, 2021. https://www.oregonlive.com/news/2021/03/knights-university-of-oregon -donations-push-1-billion-mark-with-new-hayward-field-project.html (June 14, 2023).

Marcus, Jon. "High-Paying Jobs That Don't Need a College Degree? Thousands of Them Sit Empty." *NPR*. February 14, 2023. https://www.npr.org/2023/02/14/1155405249/high-paying-jobs-that-dont-need-a-college-degree-thousands-of-them-are-sitting-e (June 21, 2023).

Masterson, Victoria. "These Are the Degrees That Will Earn You the Most Money When You Graduate—and the Ones That Won't." *World Economic Forum*. October 28, 2021. https://www.weforum.org/agenda/2021/10/stem-degrees-most-valuable/#:~:text=The%20top%2025%20college%20degrees%20by%20pay%20and,least%20valuable%20degrees%2C%20with%20average%20pay%20of%20%2435%2C500 (June 13, 2023).

Mayer, Grace Mayer. "Culinary, Mechanics, and Construction Trade Programs Increase College Enrollment Decreases, Study Finds." *Business Insider*. April 20, 2023. https://www.businessinsider.com/culinary-mechanics-construction-trade-program-increase-college-enrollment-decreases-study-2023-4 (June 21, 2023).

McGreevy, John T. "The Great Disappearing Teaching Load." *Chronicle of Higher Education*. February 3, 2019. https://www.chronicle.com/article/the-great-disappearing-teaching-load/?resetPassword=true&email=anna%40education-rethink.com&success=true&bc_nonce=v91l22hry8bgtij4z01g6&cid=gen_sign_in (June 21, 2023).

McGurran, Brianna. "College Tuition Inflation: A Historical Perspective." *Forbes*. May 9, 2023. https://www.forbes.com/advisor/student-loans/college-tuition-inflation (June 14, 2023).

Mearian, Lucas. "Companies Move to Drop College Degree Requirements for New Hires, Focus on Skills." *Computerworld*. August 10, 2022. https://www.computerworld.com/article/3669412/companies-move-to-drop-college-degree-requirements-for-new-hires-focus-on-skills.html (June 19, 2023).

"Measuring the Most Important Outcomes of Higher Education." *Gallup-Purdue Index, Purdue Marketing and Media*. n.d. https://www.purdue.edu/newsroom/gallup (June 25, 2023).

"Michigan Technological University Overall Rankings | US News Best Colleges." *U.S. News & World Report*. n.d. https://www.usnews.com/best-colleges/michigan-tech-2292/overall-rankings#:~:text=Michigan%20Technological%20University%20is%20ranked,about%20how%20we%20rank%20schools (June 14, 2023).

Mimaroglu, Alp. "How Jack Ma Overcame His 7 Biggest Failures." *Entrepreneur*. September 9, 2016. https://www.entrepreneur.com/leadership/how -jack-ma-overcame-his-7-biggest-failures/275969 (June 9, 2023).

Mintzer, Ally. "Paying Attention: The Attention Economy." *Berkeley Economic Review*. March 31, 2020. https://econreview.berkeley.edu/paying-attention -the-attention-economy (June 19, 2023).

Misner, Ivan. "Networking Is More about Farming Than It Is about Hunting." *Dr. Ivan Misner®*. July 30, 2020. https://ivanmisner.com/networking-is -more-about-farming-than-it-is-about-hunting (June 14, 2023).

Moody, Josh. "Colleges That Received the Most Applications." *U.S. News & World Report*. October 19, 2021. https://www.usnews.com/education /best-colleges/the-short-list-college/articles/colleges-that-received-the-most -applications (July 3, 2023).

Morse, Robert, and Eric Brooks. "A More Detailed Look at the Ranking Factors." *U.S. News & World Report*. September 12, 2022. https://www.usnews .com/education/best-colleges/articles/ranking-criteria-and-weights #:~:text=To%20most%20accurately%20represent%20the,effect%20on%20 that%20school's%20ranking (June 6, 2023).

Motzkin, Lauren. "Expenses a Concern for Arts Majors." *Yale Daily News*. November 10, 2012. https://yaledailynews.com/blog/2009/11/20/expenses -a-concern-for-arts-majors (June 15, 2023).

Najarro, Ileana. "States Are Mandating Asian American Studies. What Should the Curriculum Look Like?" *Education Week*. November 29, 2022. https:// www.edweek.org/teaching-learning/states-are-mandating-asian-american -studies-what-should-the-curriculum-look-like/2022/10 (June 13, 2023).

Ng, David. "Obama Shows His Support for National Arts and Humanities Month." *Los Angeles Times*. October 4, 2010. https://www.latimes.com /archives/blogs/culture-monster-blog/story/2010-10-04/obama-shows-his -support-for-national-arts-and-humanities-month#:~:text=A%20PROCLA MATION%20Throughout%20history%2C%20the%20arts%20and%20 humanities,us%20and%20reminding%20us%20of%20our%20shared%20 humanity (June 13, 2023).

"Noel Quinn." *HSBC Holdings Plc*. n.d. https://www.hsbc.com/who-we-are /leadership-and-governance/board-of-directors/noel-quinn (June 16, 2023).

"OES Home." *U.S. Bureau of Labor Statistics*. April 25, 2023. https://www .bls.gov/oes/#:~:text=The%20Occupational%20Employment%20and%20

Wage,annually%20for%20approximately%20830%20occupations (June 15, 2023).

"Oprah Winfrey: Passion Is Energy." *Bloomberg*. October 15, 2015. https:// www.bloomberg.com/news/videos/2015-10-15/oprah-winfrey-passion-is -energy (June 16, 2023).

O'Shaughnessy, Lynn. "Why Don't Professors Like to Teach?" *CBS News*. December 20, 2010. https://www.cbsnews.com/news/why-dont-professors -like-to-teach (June 23, 2023).

Park, Alice. "Google's AI Will Now Be Used in Mammograms." *Time*. November 28, 2022. https://time.com/6237088/mammograms-google-ai (June 13, 2023).

"Partnerships." *Embry-Riddle Aeronautical University*. n.d. https://erau.edu /partnerships#:~:text=Embry%2DRiddle%20partners%20with%20 the,FAA)%2C%20and%20Diamond%20Aircraft (June 14, 2023).

Paterson, James. "Moody's: Slow Enrollment Gains Raise Colleges' Financial Risk." *Higher Ed Dive*. March 7, 2019. https://www.highereddive.com/news /moodys-slow-enrollment-gains-raise-colleges-financial-risk/549960 (June 21, 2023).

"Portland State Athletics Unveils New Logo and Branding." *Portland State University Athletics*. May 19, 2016. https://goviks.com/news/2016/5/19 /portland-state-athletics-with-help-from-nike-unveils-new-logo-and -branding.aspx#:~:text=Portland%20State%20University%2C%20in%20 partnership,PSU%20Athletic%20Director%20Mark%20Rountree%20 (June 14, 2023).

"Program Details | UCLA Extension." *UCLA Extension*. n.d. https://www .uclaextension.edu/study-abroad-programs/program-details#:~:text=Full %2Dtime%20enrollment&text=Most%20UCLA%20and%20UCLA%20 Extension,course%20load%20for%20most%20students (June 2, 2023).

"Public School Enrollment." *National Center for Education Statistics*. May 2023. https://nces.ed.gov/programs/coe/indicator/cga/public-school-enroll ment (June 19, 2023).

"Quote of the Day Archives." *Wheaton College*. n.d. https://www.wheaton.edu /life-at-wheaton/kingdom-diversity/quote-of-the-day-archives (June 5, 2023).

Robby. "Cornell University: 2023 Requirements, Scores & GPAs." *Education Today*. April 3, 2023. https://educationtodaynews.net/cornell-university -acceptance-rate-gpa (June 15, 2023).

Rometty, Ginni. "6 Lessons I Learned Building a Culture That Recruits for 'Skills First' Not Just Degrees." *LinkedIn.* n.d. https://www.linkedin.com /pulse/6-lessons-i-learned-building-culture-recruits-skills-first-rometty (June 15, 2023).

Rose, Tara A., and Terri L. Flateby. "From College to Career Success." *Inside Higher Ed.* July 14, 2022. https://www.insidehighered.com/views /2022/07/15/employers-recent-grads-rate-their-skills-opinion (June 24, 2023).

Rosenberg, John S. "Harvard Admits Record-Low 5.2 Percent of Applicants to Class of 2020." *Harvard Magazine.* April 1, 2016. https://www .harvardmagazine.com/2016/04/harvard-accepts-record-low-5-2-percent -of-applicants-to-class-of-2020#:~:text=Harvard%20Admits%20 Record%2DLow%205.2%20Percent%20of%20Applicants%20to%20 Class%20of%202020&text=Harvard%20College%20announced%20 today%20that,granted%20early%2Daction%20admission (June 5, 2023).

Rudulph, Heather Wood. "Get That Life: How I Became a Professional Pastry Chef." *Cosmopolitan.* November 1, 2021. https://www.cosmopolitan.com /career/a59847/caroline-schiff-greene-grape-get-that-life (June 19, 2023).

Saadah, Yezen. "NYU Acceptance Rate Drops to 8% for Class of 2027." *Washington Square News.* March 29, 2023. https://nyunews.com/news/2023/03/29 /nyu-admission-rate-class-of-2027 (June 5, 2023).

"Salary: Entry-Level Reporter in United States June 2023." *Glassdoor.* n.d. https://www.glassdoor.com/Salaries/entry-level-reporter-salary-SRCH _KO0,20.htm (July 5, 2023).

Sanchez, Olivia. "Why Many Students Are Choosing Trade Programs over College." *Christian Science Monitor.* April 21, 2023. https://www.csmonitor .com/USA/Education/2023/0417/Why-many-students-are-choosing-trade -programs-over-college (June 21, 2023).

Saul, Derek. "NBA Docks Mavericks $750,000 for Tanking—Just .01% of Billionaire Owner Mark Cuban's Net Worth." *Forbes.* April 14, 2023. https://www.forbes.com/sites/dereksaul/2023/04/14/nba-docks-mavericks -750000-for-tanking-just-0001-of-billionaire-owner-mark-cubans-net -worth/?sh=347362296f0f (June 16, 2023).

Schacter, Laura M. "Race, Criminal Justice, and Migration Control: Enforcing the Boundaries of Belonging." *Michigan Law Review* 115, no. 8 (June 2017):

1315–70. https://repository.law.umich.edu/cgi/viewcontent.cgi?params
=/context/mlr/article/5435/&path_info= (June 13, 2023).

Schroeder, Ray. "Colleges Should Be Planning More Intentionally for Students Who Commute to Campuses This Fall." *Inside Higher Ed.* July 23, 2020. https://www.insidehighered.com/views/2020/07/23/colleges-should-be-planning-more-intentionally-students-who-commute-campuses-fall (June 21, 2023).

Schwartz, Barry. *The Paradox of Choice: Why More Is Less.* 2004. https://changethis.com/manifesto/13.ParadoxOfChoice/pdf/13.ParadoxOfChoice.pdf (June 13, 2023).

"See Where Michigan Technological University Ranks among the World's Best Universities." *U.S. News & World Report.* n.d. https://www.usnews.com/education/best-global-universities/michigan-technological-university-171128 (June 14, 2023).

Segal, Gillian Zoe. "This Self-Made Billionaire Failed the LSAT Twice, Then Sold Fax Machines for 7 Years before Hitting Big—Here's How She Got There." *CNBC.* April 3, 2019. https://www.cnbc.com/2019/04/03/self-made-billionaire-spanx-founder-sara-blakely-sold-fax-machines-before-making-it-big.html (June 12, 2023).

"SOC2019: State of College Admission." *National Association for College Admission Counseling.* n.d. https://nacacnet.org/wp-content/uploads/2022/10/soca2019_all.pdf (June 15, 2023).

Speakman, Kimberlee. "New Orleans High School Student Receives Record $9M in Scholarship Offers from 125 Colleges." *People.* April 25, 2023. https://people.com/human-interest/new-orleans-high-school-student-receives-record-9m-in-scholarship-offers-from-125-colleges (June 22, 2023).

Staff Reporter. "John Legend: My Success Is Due to the Teachers Who Believed in Me." *HuffPost UK* (blog). November 8, 2017. https://www.huffingtonpost.co.uk/entry/level-playing-field-for-students_uk_5c7e9943e4b048b41e3a2d99 (June 13, 2023).

"State of the Humanities 2021: Workforce & Beyond." *American Academy of Arts & Sciences.* March 10, 2023. https://www.amacad.org/publication humanities-workforce-beyond (June 11, 2023).

Stokes, Kris. "Closing the Skills Gap 2023." *Wiley.* January 24, 2023. https://universityservices.wiley.com/closing-the-skills-gap-2023 (June 21, 2023).

Stolzenberg, Ellen Bara, Melissa C. Aragon, Edgar Romo, Victoria Couch, Destiny McLennan, M. Kevin Eagan, and Nathaniel Kang. "The American Freshman: National Norms Fall 2019." *Higher Education Research Institute*, Monograph Series, 2020. https://www.heri.ucla.edu/monographs/The AmericanFreshman2019.pdf (June 19, 2023).

"Student Debt and the Class of 2020." *The Institute for College Access & Success.* November 2021. https://ticas.org/wp-content/uploads/2021/11/classof2020 .pdf (June 21, 2023).

"Survey of Household Economics and Decisionmaking." *Federal Reserve.* n.d. https://www.federalreserve.gov/consumerscommunities/shed.htm (June 15, 2023).

"10 Facts about Today's College Graduates." *Pew Research Center.* n.d. https:// www.pewresearch.org/short-reads/2022/04/12/10-facts-about-todays-col lege-graduates.

"The Best Undergraduate Teaching National Universities." *U.S. News & World Report.* n.d. https://www.usnews.com/best-colleges/rankings/national-uni versities/undergraduate-teaching (June 21, 2023).

"The Best Universities in China, Ranked." n.d. https://www.usnews.com/edu cation/best-global-universities/china?city=hangzhou (June 1, 2023).

"The Best Universities in the World, Ranked." n.d. https://www.usnews.com /education/best-global-universities/rankings (June 9, 2023).

"The Common App Is a Broken, Bloated Monopoly." *New York Times.* March 16, 2023. https://www.nytimes.com/2023/03/16/opinion/college -admissions-common-app.html (June 20, 2023).

"The Economic Value of College Majors." *Georgetown University Center on Education and the Workforce.* n.d. https://cew.georgetown.edu/cew-reports /valueofcollegemajors (June 21, 2023).

"The Foundation for Sound Journalism, Whether You're a Budding Journalist or a Seasoned One Looking for a Refresher." *Reuters.* May 18, 2021. https:// www.reutersagency.com/pt-br/media-center/reuters-launches-the-reuters -digital-journalism-course-in-partnership-with-the-facebook-journalism-pro ject (June 15, 2023).

"The Top Ten Richest People in the World." *Forbes.* June 1, 2023. https:// www.forbes.com/sites/forbeswealthteam/article/the-top-ten-richest-people -in-the-world/?sh=704792e354dc (June 13, 2023).

"Top College Rankings List 2017: US News Investigation." *Politico*. n.d. https://www.politico.com/interactives/2017/top-college-rankings-list -2017-us-news-investigation (June 14, 2023).

"Transfer Requirements." *University of California Admissions*. n.d. https:// admission.universityofcalifornia.edu/admission-requirements/transfer -requirements (June 20, 2023).

Tugend, Alina. "Who Benefits from the Expansion of AP Classes?" *New York Times*. September 7, 2017. https://www.nytimes.com/2017/09/07/magazine /who-benefits-from-the-expansion-of-ap-classes.html (July 5, 2023).

"Tuition & Aid." *UCLA Undergraduate Admission*. n.d. https://admission.ucla .edu/tuition-aid (July 3, 2023).

"Tuition and Fees." *Amherst College*. n.d. https://www.amherst.edu/tuition (June 20, 2023).

"Tuition Discount Rates at Private Colleges and Universities Hit All-Time Highs." *Nacubo*. May 19, 2022. https://www.nacubo.org/Press-Releases/2022 /Tuition%20Discount%20Rates%20at%20Private%20Colleges%20and%20 Universities%20Hit%20All%20Time%20Highs#:~:text=In%20AY%20 2021-22%2C%2082.5%20percent%20of%20all%20undergraduates,of%20 60.7%20percent%20of%20published%20tuition%20and%20fees (June 15, 2023).

"Tuition Rates and Fees." *Cornell University Division of Financial Affairs*. n.d. https://www.dfa.cornell.edu/bursar/students-parents/tuition-rates-fees (June 14, 2023).

Twenge, Jean, Wendy Wang, Jenet Erickson, and Brad Wilcox. "Teens and Tech: What Difference Does Family Structure Make?" *Institute for Family Studies*. October 2022. https://ifstudies.org/ifs-admin/resources/reports /teensandtech-final-1.pdf (June 10, 2023).

"UC Berkeley Quick Facts." *Office of Planning and Analysis, UC Berkeley*. n.d. https://opa.berkeley.edu/campus-data/uc-berkeley-quick-facts (June 14, 2023).

"Undergraduate Enrollment." *National Center for Education Statistics*. May 2023. https://nces.ed.gov/programs/coe/indicator/cha/undergrad -enrollment#:~:text=Between%20fall%202010%20and%20fall,percent%20 to%2016.8%20million%20students (June 28, 2023).

"US News Best Colleges." *U.S. News & World Report*. n.d. https://www.us news.com/best-colleges (June 13, 2023).

Van Dam, Andrew. "The Most-Regretted (and Lowest-Paying) College Majors." *Washington Post*. September 2, 2022. https://www.washingtonpost.com/business/2022/09/02/college-major-regrets (June 21, 2023).

Van Rijswijk, Lotte. "The Happiest Schools in the U.S., UK and Australia." *Resume.io*. March 22, 2023. https://resume.io/blog/the-happiest-schools-in-the-us-uk-and-australia (June 14, 2023).

Vazquez, Ricardo. "UCLA Applications for Fall 2023 Admission Remain at Near-Historic Highs." *UCLA*. February 24, 2023. https://newsroom.ucla.edu/releases/ucla-applications-for-fall-2023-admissions (June 4, 2023).

Vigil, Joe. "Southern Nevada Has 8 Years of Water Reserves as State Faces Water Cuts from Colorado River." *Fox 5*. August 20, 2022. https://www.fox5vegas.com/2022/08/20/southern-nevada-has-eight-years-water-reserves-nevada-faces-water-shortage-cuts-colorado-river (June 13, 2023).

Walker, Ezekiel J. "ATL Teen Accepted by 50+ Colleges with $1.3 Million in Scholarships." *Black Wall Street Times*. March 15, 2023. https://theblackwallsttimes.com/2023/03/15/atl-teen-accepted-by-50-colleges-with-1-3-million-in-scholarships (June 4, 2023).

Waltower, Shayna. "The Skills Gap Is Costing Businesses Dearly." *Business News Daily*. February 21, 2023. https://www.businessnewsdaily.com/6038-skills-gaps-cost-companies-thousands.html (June 14, 2023).

Watanabe, Teresa. "UC Applications Slow Down for Fall 2023 with Drop in Out-of-State Students." *Los Angeles Times*. February 24, 2023. https://www.latimes.com/california/story/2023-02-24/uc-applications-slow-down-for-fall-2023-with-drop-in-out-of-state-students (June 4, 2023).

Watson, Anna. "Ranking the Top Schools for a Career in Marketing." *Poets&Quants for Undergrads*. April 2, 2023. https://poetsandquantsforundergrads.com/uncategorized/ranking-the-top-schools-for-a-career-in-marketing/#:~:text=The%20University%20of%20Wisconsin%20at,new%20ranking%20from%20BookYourDbestata.com (June 13, 2023).

White, Scott. "Benefits of Attending a Less Selective College." *College Solution*. n.d. https://thecollegesolution.com/benefits-of-attending-a-less-selective-college (June 21, 2023).

Wilkie, Dana. "Employers Say Students Aren't Learning Soft Skills in College." *Society for Human Resource Management*. October 21, 2019. https://www.shrm.org/resourcesandtools/hr-topics/employee-relations/pages/employers-say-students-arent-learning-soft-skills-in-college.aspx (June 13, 2023).

Winters, Mike. "The 10 Highest-Paying College Majors, Five Years after Graduation." *CNBC*. February 20, 2023. https://www.cnbc.com/2023/02/20/highest-paying-college-majors.html (June 13, 2023).

Winters, Mike. "The Worst Paying College Majors, Five Years after Graduation." *CNBC*. February 25, 2023. https://www.cnbc.com/2023/02/25/worst-paying-college-majors.html#:~:text=Graduates%20who%20major%20in%20theology,just%20over%20%2417%20per%20hour (June 13, 2023).

Wood, Sarah. "Colleges with the Highest Application Fees." *U.S. News & World Report*. January 28, 2022. https://www.usnews.com/education/best-colleges/the-short-list-college/articles/colleges-with-the-highest-application-fees (June 13, 2023).

York, Joanna. "Does Doing What You Love for a Living Come with a Price?" *BBC Worklife*. February 25, 2022. https://www.bbc.com/worklife/article/20210927-does-doing-what-you-love-for-a-living-come-with-a-price (June 13, 2023).

Young, Christal. "Museum of Failure Exhibit Opens in Brooklyn." *Fox 5 New York*. April 1, 2023. https://www.fox5ny.com/news/museum-of-failure-nyc-brooklyn-open-march-may-14 (June 16, 2023).

Yu, Yi-Jin. "High Schooler Accepted into 72 Colleges Shares Advice for Other Students." *Good Morning America*. April 27, 2022. https://www.goodmorningamerica.com/living/story/high-schooler-accepted-72-colleges-shares-advice-students-84325285#:~:text=Ja'Leaha%20Thornton%20of%20Belle,from%2072%20schools%20and%20counting (June 4, 2023).

Zaretsky, Staci. "Ranking the Most 'Devout' Law Schools (2023)." *Above the Law*. March 21, 2023. https://abovethelaw.com/2023/03/ranking-the-most-devout-law-schools-2023 (June 13, 2023).

INDEX

ABOUT THE AUTHOR

Anna Esaki-Smith is a writer and education researcher. As a journalist, she has lived and worked in Hong Kong, Shanghai, Paris, and Tokyo. She raised her two sons overseas and currently lives with her husband in Chappaqua, New York.